The Art of
South American
Cookery

D0167698

HIPPOCRENE INTERNATIONAL COOKBOOK SERIES

The Cuisine of Armenia
A Belgian Cookbook
The Art of Brazilian Cookery
The Best of Czech Cooking
Traditional Recipes of Old England
The Best of Finnish Cooking
The Art of Hungarian Cooking
The Art of Irish Cooking
The Art Israeli Cooking
The Art of Persian Cooking
Old Warsaw Cookbook
The Best of Polish Cooking
Polish Heritage Cookery
Old Polish Traditions in the Kitchen
The Best of Russian Cooking
Traditional Food from Scotland
Traditional South African Cookery
The Art of South American Cookery
A Spanish Family Cookbook
The Best of Smorgasbord Cooking
Good Food from Sweden
The Art of Turkish Cooking
The Best of Ukrainian Cuisine
All Along the Danube

MYRA WALDO

The Art of
South American
Cookery

Illustrated by
JOHN ALCORN

HIPPOCRENE BOOKS
New York

Originally published by Doubleday & Company,
New York.

Hippocrene paperback edition, 1996.

For information, address:
HIPPOCRENE BOOKS
171 Madison Avenue
New York, NY 10016

Library of Congress Cataloging-in-Publication Data
Waldo, Myra.
        The art of South American cookery / Myra Waldo.--
Hippocrene pbk. ed.
            p.   cm
        Includes index.
        ISBN 0-7818-0485-X
        1. Cookery, Latin American. 2. Cookery--South America.
    I. Title.
    TX716.A1W35   1996   96-21463
    641.598--dc20   CIP

Printed in the United States of America.

Contents

Recipes capitalized in the text may be located by
consulting the Index.

Introduction

To our south lies the vast, complex area of South America, a continent of seemingly boundless distances. It offers much to the tourist, and to the gourmet too. For South American food is amazingly good—a complete, almost undiscovered cookery style. As a rule it is mild and no more highly seasoned than American food. The myth that Latin dishes are spicy is probably based upon the reports of those who have sampled only the Mexican cuisine, which often, although not always, overdoes the use of hot ingredients. Rest assured, the overwhelming majority of South American dishes have the great merit of being readily prepared and immediately enjoyed.

The food of continental Europe has always been recognized and approved of by Americans; the past years have seen the acceptance of Oriental styles of cooking. Probably this is because most American tourists have visited Europe and the Orient, whereas comparatively few have explored the fascinating countries of South America. By not visiting that long continent, tourists have missed a great deal—a marvelous area filled with delightful things to see and do, and wonderful food.

It should also be mentioned that occasionally in this book the names of dishes will appear with similar but slightly different spellings. This is not accidental: both Spanish and Portuguese are spoken in South America, and although the languages are similar, there are variations. In addition, many local dialects have modified the classic names and spelling. Further, the translations supplied for many of the dishes are intentionally not always literal or exact, since many such translations would fail to explain the nature of the dish.

9

Parts of South America have very similar cookery styles. For example, many countries serve the classic dishes brought from their motherlands: Spain and Portugal. However, the locally available ingredients have naturally influenced and modified the cuisines of the individual countries. Chile, for example, has taken full advantage of its long coastline and superb fisheries to create some delectable seafood preparations. Notable is *Chupe de Mariscos*, a seafood soup-stew or chowder. Brazil, using the black beans of the country, has as its national dish *Feijoada*, made with beans and a variety of meats and spices. Argentina, a great meat country, combines meats with fruits and vegetables, resulting in a *Carbonada*. One of Peru's contributions to the art of good eating is a marvelous chicken-and-pepper dish called *Ají de Pollo*. Dishes with *Salsa de Almendras*, almond sauce, are familiar through large parts of South America, but reach a high point of deliciousness in Ecuador, where this sauce is served with shrimp, eggs, and almost anything the chef has available.

You will find that cooking the South American way introduces a new type of cuisine into your menu. It offers a scope and excitement that will delight your family and guests.

Myra Waldo

APPETIZERS

APPETIZERS

In South America most people enjoy meals of several courses, and a repast without an appetizer course would be unthinkable. A one-course casserole meal in the familiar American fashion would make no headway whatsoever with our neighbors to the south. They like elaborate meals, and are particularly fond of beginning a dinner with something spicy.

In Argentina and Chile, for example, the meal might well begin with *Seviche* or *Escabeche*, the delicately pickled fish or poultry preparations intended to pique the appetite. For Americans, an interesting appetizer plate might be arranged, consisting of an assortment of several South American first-course preparations. One idea might be to combine small portions of Mexican *Guacamole*, avocado mix, *Seviche*, marinated fish, *Escabeche*, and an *Empanada*, stuffed pastry, on one plate; this will surely be an interesting beginning to a meal, certain to be a conversation piece. Incidentally, many of the appetizers in this section are ideal as cocktail accompaniments.

Croquetes de Camarões

SHRIMP CROQUETTES

1 pound raw shrimp, shelled and deveined
2 tablespoons butter
¾ cup finely chopped onions
1 clove garlic, minced
1 slice white bread
¼ cup milk
1 tablespoon minced parsley
1½ teaspoons salt
¼ teaspoon freshly ground black pepper
2 eggs
½ cup dry bread crumbs
¼ cup salad oil

Chop the shrimp very fine. Melt the butter in a skillet; sauté the onions and garlic until golden-brown. Soak the bread in the milk; drain and mash smooth. Mix together the shrimp, bread, sautéed onions, parsley, salt, pepper, and 1 egg. Form heaping tablespoons of the mixture into croquettes (if too loose to hold shape, add a little flour). Beat remaining egg, dip croquettes in it, then in bread crumbs.

Heat the oil in a skillet and fry the croquettes until browned on both sides. Makes about 10.

On Chile's west coast is the large, progressive city of Valparaiso. It is interestingly situated, facing a rather large bay open to the sea; breakwaters have been constructed to prevent the destruction of harbor facilities, which formerly occurred when fierce storms drove in from the South Pacific. Valparaiso means Vale of Paradise, a rather fanciful name, but one that might be justified because of this city's unusually favorable climate. The city is built on two levels, the lower part being used principally for business and the upper portion primarily for residences. Public elevators are used to connect the two parts of the city.

Not too far north of Valparaiso is Chile's favorite resort city of Viña del Mar, or Vineyard by the Sea. It is a lovely region, with seaside hotels, a gambling casino, race track, and other amenities of continental resort life. Many people compare it favorably to portions of the French Riviera for climate, scenery, and accommodations. Just to the north of Viña del Mar runs the road to Concón; along the road, which closely follows the sea, are innumerable charming restaurants perched on the rocks over the ocean and featuring the many delicious fish and shellfish of the region.

 Emparedados

SEAFOOD-COCKTAIL SANDWICHES

1½ cups cooked shrimp, lobster, or crab meat
⅛ teaspoon Tabasco
3 tablespoons minced onions
2 tablespoons minced parsley
2 tablespoons mayonnaise
12 thin slices white bread
1 cup milk
2 eggs
½ cup flour
½ teaspoon salt
Fat for deep frying

Chop together until very fine the seafood, Tabasco, onions, and parsley; blend in the mayonnaise. Trim the bread and cut in half. Dry in the oven without browning. Dip lightly in the milk (reserve leftover milk) and spread half the pieces with the seafood mixture. Make sandwiches, pressing the edges together.

Beat together the eggs, flour, salt, and remaining milk. Dip the sandwiches in the batter. Heat the fat to 370° and fry the sandwiches until browned. Drain and serve hot. Makes a dozen.

🐟 *Camarones Con Salsa de Almendras*

SHRIMP IN ALMOND SAUCE

1½ *cups water*
1 *stalk celery*
½ *teaspoon pickling spice*
2 *teaspoons salt*
2 *pounds raw shrimp, shelled and deveined*
1½ *cups diced white bread*
1½ *cups milk*
4 *tablespoons butter*
1½ *cups finely chopped onions*
2 *cloves garlic, minced*
½ *teaspoon freshly ground black pepper*
¼ *teaspoon dried ground chili peppers*
1 *teaspoon Spanish paprika*
½ *cup olive oil*
1 *cup ground almonds*

Bring the water, celery, pickling spice, and 1 teaspoon salt to a boil. Add the shrimp and cook over medium heat for 7 minutes. Drain, reserving 1 cup stock.

Soak the bread in the milk for 10 minutes and mash smooth. Do not drain. Melt the butter in a skillet; sauté the onions and garlic until soft and browned. Mix in the pepper, chili peppers, paprika, and undrained bread; sauté for 5 minutes, stirring frequently. Gradually mix in the olive oil, then the almonds and remaining salt; cook for 2 minutes. Blend in the stock and add the shrimp; cook over low heat for 5 minutes. Taste for seasoning. Serves 6–8, as a first course.

Picante de Aguacates

AVOCADO APPETIZER

3 avocados
6 hard-cooked egg yolks
2 canned chilis Jalapeños, or ½ teaspoon dried ground
  chili peppers
¼ cup finely chopped onions
3 tablespoons minced parsley
2 tablespoons cider vinegar
1½ teaspoons salt

Peel the avocados and chop fine with the egg yolks, chili peppers, onions, and parsley. Mix in the vinegar and salt. Taste for seasoning. Serve in a bowl as a dip with Fritos, potato chips, or toast. Or serve on lettuce as an appetizer. Makes about 3 cups.

 Huevos Picantes

SARDINE STUFFED EGGS

8 hard-cooked eggs
8 skinless and boneless sardines
2 tablespoons grated onions
2 tablespoons ketchup
2 tablespoons mayonnaise
2 pimientos, cut julienne

Cut the eggs in half lengthwise and scoop out the yolks. Mash smooth with the sardines, onions, ketchup, and mayonnaise. Stuff the whites and arrange the pimientos on top. Makes 16.

Guacamole is a spicy avocado dish that is extremely popular in Mexico and some South American countries. It is prepared in several different fashions, according to varying local recipes. These are all interesting; serve as a dip, spread, or salad.

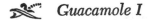 *Guacamole I*

AVOCADO DIP

2 *avocados*
2 *tomatoes, peeled and chopped*
¼ *cup minced onions*
1 *teaspoon salt*
2 *teaspoons chili powder*
2 *teaspoons lemon juice*

Scoop out the pulp of the avocados and mash smooth. Mix with the tomatoes, onions, salt, chili powder, and lemon juice. Taste for seasoning. Serve with Fritos, potato chips, or *tortillas*. Makes about 2 cups.

Guacamole II

AVOCADO DIP

2 *avocados*
3 *tablespoons grated onions*
2 *tablespoons minced, canned Jalapeños peppers*
1 *teaspoon salt*
1 *tablespoon lemon juice*

Cut the avocados in half lengthwise and scoop out the pulp. Mash until smooth and blend in the onions, peppers, salt, and lemon juice. Taste for seasoning and serve with *tortillas*, Fritos, or toast. Makes about 2 cups.

Guacamole III

AVOCADO DIP

2 *avocados*
4 *anchovies, minced*
4 *tablespoons minced scallions (green onions)*
1½ *tablespoons lime or lemon juice*
¼ *teaspoon Tabasco*

Cut the avocados in half lengthwise and scoop out the pulp. Chop fine; blend with the anchovies, scallions, lime juice, and Tabasco. Taste for seasoning. Makes about 2 cups.

 Picante de Abacate

AVOCADO-SALAD APPETIZER

This recipe was furnished by Panagra's Commissary in Santiago, Chile.

½ *cup olive oil*
3 *tablespoons wine vinegar*
1 *clove garlic, minced*
1 *teaspoon salt*
½ *teaspoon freshly ground black pepper*
½ *teaspoon sugar*
¼ *cup finely chopped scallions (green onions)*
1 *tablespoon minced parsley*
2 *tablespoons chopped capers*
3 *avocados, peeled and sliced thin*

In a salad bowl, beat together the oil, vinegar, garlic, salt, pepper, and sugar. Add the scallions, parsley, capers, and avocados; toss until well coated. Chill for 1 hour before serving. Serves 4–6.

Carnitas

FRIED PORK BITS

2 pounds fat pork
1½ cups water
2 teaspoons salt
½ teaspoon dried ground chili peppers
¼ teaspoon ground cumin

Cut the pork in bite-sized cubes. Combine in a skillet with the water, salt, chili peppers, and cumin. Bring to a boil, cover, and cook over high heat until the water is evaporated. Remove cover and cook pork until browned and crisp. Pierce with cocktail picks and serve with a spicy sauce as a dip, if desired. Makes about 3 dozen.

 Coctel de Aguacate

AVOCADO COCKTAIL

½ cup heavy cream
½ cup chili sauce
2 tablespoons minced onions
1 tablespoon lime or lemon juice
1 teaspoon salt
Dash Tabasco
1 teaspoon Worcestershire sauce
3 avocados

Mix together the cream, chili sauce, onions, lime juice, salt, Tabasco and Worcestershire sauces. Peel and dice the avocados. Toss with the dressing. Serve in sherbet glasses or on lettuce. Serves 6.

Casquinho de Caranguejo

CRAB-MEAT RAMEKINS, Brazilian Fashion

½ cup olive oil
1 cup chopped onions
1 cup chopped green peppers
1 cup chopped tomatoes
1 clove garlic, minced
1½ teaspoons salt
½ teaspoon freshly ground black pepper
1 pound crab meat
2 tablespoons minced parsley
2 eggs, beaten
¾ cup dry bread crumbs
3 tablespoons melted butter
½ cup stuffed green olives

Heat the olive oil in a skillet; sauté the onions for 10 minutes. Mix in the green peppers, tomatoes, garlic, salt, and pepper; cook over low heat for 10 minutes. Add the crab meat and parsley; cook for 5 minutes. Stir in the eggs just until set. Taste for seasoning. Divide the mixture among 6 ramekins. Toss the bread crumbs with the melted butter and sprinkle over the crab meat. Arrange olives on top. Bake in a preheated 375° oven for 10 minutes, or until delicately browned. Serves 6.

SOUPS

SOUPS

South American soups are quite unusual, offering an almost endless succession of delightful flavors. Many of the soups are almost meals in themselves, so menus—for Americans, that is—must be balanced accordingly. Thus, if one of the heartier types of soups is being scrved, the main course should be light and comparatively simple.

Our Latin neighbors like to serve soup from tureens; the delicious contents of the tureen is ladled into deep, large soup plates or bowls, ideal for holding delectable ingredient-laden mixtures. Frequently second helpings are the rule, which should indicate how tempting South American soups can be. An outstanding example of a superb national soup is the Argentine classic, *Sopa Criolla de Pollo*, a chicken-and-vegetable soup. Mexico offers *Sopa Frijoles Rojo*, red-bean soup; Chile, *Sopa de Pescado y Almendras*, a fish-and-almond soup. But these are just a few of the really superb soups that follow.

Sopa de Albondiguillas

MEAT-BALL SOUP

½ *pound ground pork or beef*
1 *clove garlic, minced*
1 *teaspoon salt*
Dash cayenne pepper
1 *egg, beaten*
¼ *cup bottled chili sauce*
1 *tablespoon minced parsley*
½ *cup bread crumbs*
2 *tablespoons butter*
7 *cups beef broth*

Mix together the meat, garlic, salt, cayenne pepper, egg, chili sauce, and parsley. Shape into walnut-sized balls and roll in the bread crumbs. Brown in the butter, then cook in the beef broth for 20 minutes. Serves 6–8.

 Sopa de Arroz

RICE SOUP

3 *tablespoons butter*
¾ *cup chopped onions*
1½ *cups raw rice*
8 *cups hot chicken broth*
½ *teaspoon white pepper*
½ *teaspoon saffron*

Melt the butter in a saucepan; sauté the onions for 5 minutes. Stir in the rice until golden. Add half the broth and the pepper. Cover and cook over low heat for 25 minutes. Mix in the remaining broth and the saffron. Cook 10 minutes longer. Taste for seasoning. Serves 6–8.

Sopa Criolla de Pollo

ARGENTINE THICK CHICKEN-AND-VEGETABLE SOUP

This recipe was furnished by Panagra's Commissary in Buenos Aires, Argentina.

1 4-pound pullet, disjointed
5 cups water
½ cup chopped onions
2 tablespoons diced green peppers
½ cup peeled, diced tomatoes
2 cloves garlic, minced
½ cup diced carrots
1 tablespoon salt
½ teaspoon white pepper
½ cup raw rice
½ cup diced potatoes
½ cup shredded cabbage
½ cup green peas
2 tablespoons minced parsley
1 tablespoon minced cilantro—fresh coriander—(optional)

Combine the chicken, water, onions, green peppers, tomatoes, garlic, and carrots in a saucepan. Bring to a boil. Cover and cook over low heat 1¼ hours. Add the salt, pepper, rice, potatoes, cabbage, peas, parsley, and *cilantro*. Cook for 30 minutes. Taste for seasoning and serve in deep bowls. The meat can be cut from the bones before serving, if you like. Serves 4.

⚞ Mondongo

PEPPER POT

½ pound dried chick-peas
1½ pounds tripe
Veal knuckles
6 quarts water
1 lemon, sliced
½ teaspoon thyme
1 tablespoon salt
1 teaspoon freshly ground black pepper
¾ cup chopped onions
2 cloves garlic, minced
2 cups diced tomatoes
3 carrots, sliced
2 sweet potatoes, peeled and diced
1 yellow squash, cubed
2 cups shredded cabbage
2 teaspoons Worcestershire sauce

Soak the chick-peas overnight in water to cover.

Wash the tripe and cut in 1-inch-wide strips. Combine in a saucepan with the veal knuckles, 6 quarts water, and lemon. Bring to a boil and cook over low heat 4 hours. Add the drained chick-peas, the thyme, salt, pepper, onions, garlic, tomatoes, carrots, sweet potatoes, squash, and cabbage. Cover and cook over low heat 2 hours. Stir in the Worcestershire sauce. Taste for seasoning—the soup should be spicy. Serves 10–12.

Quito, capital of Ecuador, is a fascinating, rather small city of less than 100,000 people. It is situated just a few miles south of the equator, and tourists can drive out to the monument which marks the imaginary line and have their pictures taken with one foot in the Northern and one foot in the Southern Hemisphere.

 Chupe de Mariscos

CHILEAN SHRIMP-AND-SCALLOP SOUP

6 tablespoons butter
1 cup finely chopped onions
4 cups bottled clam juice
4 cups dry white wine
½ teaspoon white pepper
2 slices white bread, trimmed and diced
1 cup milk
1 pound raw shrimp, shelled and deveined
1 pound scallops
⅛ teaspoon diced ground chili peppers
½ cup ground almonds
1 cup heavy cream
½ teaspoon paprika
2 hard-cooked eggs, chopped

Melt the butter in a saucepan; sauté the onions until soft and lightly browned. Mix in the clam juice, wine, and pepper; bring to a boil and cook over low heat for 30 minutes. Soak the bread in the milk and mash smooth; add to the saucepan and cook over low heat for 10 minutes. Add the shrimp, scallops, and chili peppers. Cook for 5 minutes. Blend in the almonds, cream, paprika, and eggs. Cook 5 minutes longer. Taste for seasoning. Serves 8–10.

Sopa de Pescado y Almendras

FISH-AND-ALMOND SOUP

2 pounds fillet of red snapper or sole
1 pound raw shrimp, shelled and deveined
3 tablespoons butter
1 cup chopped onions
8 cups chicken broth
¼ pound ham, finely chopped
½ cup raw rice
1 teaspoon salt
½ teaspoon freshly ground black pepper
½ teaspoon saffron
1 cup blanched ground almonds
3 hard-cooked egg yolks, chopped
3 tablespoons minced parsley

Cut the fish and shrimp in bite-sized pieces. Melt the butter in a saucepan; sauté the onions for 10 minutes. Add the broth and ham; bring to a boil and cook over medium heat for 10 minutes. Stir in the rice, salt, pepper, saffron, and fish. Cover and cook over low heat for 20 minutes. Add the almonds and shrimp; cook 10 minutes longer. Taste for seasoning and stir in the egg yolks and parsley. Serves 8–10.

Argentina has some of the world's greatest trenchermen (and that includes women too!). A typical dinner might have the following menu:

Apéritif: *A glass of vermouth and soda*
Appetizer: Perdices en Escabeche *(pickled partridges)*
Soup: Sopa Criolla *(a type of vegetable soup)*
Fish: Filete de Pejerrey *(a local fish)*
Meat: Lomo *(much like the fillet cut of steak)*
Dessert: Dulce de Leche *(a sweet milk dessert)*
Wine: *Both white and red Argentine wines*

Potaje de Pescado

FISH SOUP

2 quarts water
1½ cups chopped onions
¼ teaspoon marjoram
½ cup chopped celery
2 pounds halibut, cod, or other white-meat fish
2 teaspoons salt
½ teaspoon freshly ground black pepper
1½ teaspoons Spanish paprika
3 tablespoons butter
3 tablespoons minced parsley
1 onion, thinly sliced
1 hard-cooked egg, grated

Combine the water, chopped onions, marjoram, and celery in a saucepan. Bring to a boil and add the fish, salt, and pepper. Cook over medium heat for 45 minutes. Mix in the paprika, butter, and parsley. Taste for seasoning. Garnish with the sliced onion and egg. Serve with croutons. Serves 6–8.

 Caldo de Pescado

FISH-AND-TOMATO BROTH

3 tablespoons olive oil
1½ cups chopped onions
2 cups chopped tomatoes
1 clove garlic, minced
1½ cups dry white wine
6 cups bottled clam juice
¼ teaspoon white pepper
2 tablespoons minced parsley

[over]

Heat the oil in a saucepan; sauté the onions until browned. Add the tomatoes and garlic; cook over low heat for 5 minutes. Add the wine, clam juice, and pepper. Cook over medium-low heat for 30 minutes. Stir in the parsley, taste for seasoning, and serve with sautéed bread. Serves 4–6.

 Albondigas al Caldillo

MEXICAN MEAT BALLS IN BROTH

2 tablespoons olive oil
3 cups chopped onions
2 cloves garlic, minced, or ½ teaspoon garlic powder
¾ cup chopped tomatoes
1 tablespoon minced parsley
1 pound ground beef
¼ cup bread crumbs
2 tablespoons water
2 eggs
1¼ teaspoons salt
½ teaspoon freshly ground black pepper
5 cups beef broth

Heat the oil in a skillet; sauté the onions for 5 minutes. Add the garlic, tomatoes, and parsley. Cook over low heat for 5 minutes. Mix with the meat, bread crumbs, water, eggs, salt, and pepper. Shape into walnut-sized balls. Drop into the boiling broth, cover, and cook over low heat for 10 minutes. Serve with rice. Serves 4–6.

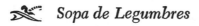 *Sopa de Legumbres*

THICK VEGETABLE SOUP

2 tablespoons olive oil
½ cup chopped onions
½ cup chopped green peppers
½ cup sliced celery
1 cup shredded cabbage
6 cups beef broth
½ teaspoon freshly ground black pepper
4 tablespoons raw rice
¾ cup cooked or canned kidney beans

Heat the oil in a saucepan; sauté the onions and green peppers for 5 minutes. Add the celery and cabbage; sauté for 5 minutes. Stir in the broth, pepper, and rice. Cover and cook over low heat for 20 minutes. Add the beans and cook 10 minutes longer. Taste for seasoning. Serves 4–6.

 Sopa de Cebollas y Almendras

ONION-ALMOND SOUP

4 tablespoons butter
5 cups chopped onions
8 cups beef broth
½ teaspoon freshly ground black pepper
1½ cups blanched ground almonds
Toasted French bread
1 cup grated Gruyère or Swiss cheese

Melt the butter in a saucepan; sauté the onions over low heat until browned and soft. Add the broth, pepper, and almonds; cook over medium heat 15 minutes longer. Taste for seasoning. Sprinkle the toast with cheese and place a slice in each plate. Pour the soup over it. Serves 6–8.

Sopa Verde

GREEN SOUP

3 tablespoons butter
1 cup chopped scallions (green onions)
2 leeks, chopped
3 cups shredded lettuce
¼ cup minced parsley
1 potato, sliced
6 cups chicken broth
¼ teaspoon white pepper
2 egg yolks
¼ cup heavy cream

Melt the butter in a saucepan; stir in the scallions, leeks, lettuce, and parsley until wilted. Add the potato, broth, and pepper. Bring to a boil and cook over low heat 25 minutes. Purée in an electric blender or force through a sieve.

Beat the egg yolks and cream in a bowl; gradually add a little hot soup, stirring steadily to prevent curdling. Return to balance of soup. Heat, but do not let boil. Taste for seasoning. Serves 6–8.

Sopa de Cebolla

ONION SOUP

2 tablespoons olive oil
3 cups thinly sliced onions
1 clove garlic, minced, or ¼ teaspoon garlic powder
6 cups beef broth
¼ teaspoon white pepper
2 egg yolks
1 teaspoon lemon juice

Heat the oil in a saucepan; sauté the onions until very brown. Add the garlic, broth, and pepper. Cook over low heat for 30 minutes. Taste for seasoning. Beat the egg yolks and lemon juice in a tureen or bowl. Pour the hot soup into it, stirring steadily. Serve with toasted French bread. Serves 6–8.

✺ *Potaje de Guisantes*

PEA SOUP

2 cups split peas
1 onion, sliced
1 carrot, sliced
2 cloves garlic, minced
1 bay leaf
9 cups water
1 package frozen chopped spinach
3 tablespoons olive oil
1½ cups chopped onions
1 cup peeled, chopped tomatoes
¼ teaspoon basil
2 tablespoons minced parsley
2 teaspoons salt
½ teaspoon freshly ground black pepper
2 hard-cooked eggs, chopped

Wash the split peas; combine with the sliced onion, carrot, garlic, bay leaf, and water. Bring to a boil; add the spinach and cook over low heat for 1½ hours, or until tender. Purée in an electric blender or force through a sieve.

Heat the oil in a skillet; sauté the chopped onions until browned. Add the tomatoes, basil, parsley, salt, and pepper. Cook over low heat for 5 minutes. Add to the soup. Cook for 20 minutes. Taste for seasoning; serve with the chopped eggs on top. Serves 6–8.

Puré de Garbanzos

CREAM OF CHICK-PEA SOUP

1½ cups dried chick-peas
8 cups water
½ cup chopped onions
2 teaspoons salt
½ teaspoon freshly ground black pepper
2 cups light cream

Wash the chick-peas and cover with water. Bring to a boil; let soak for 1 hour. Drain, add the water and the onions. Cook over medium-low heat for 2 hours. Purée in an electric blender or force through a sieve. Stir in the salt, pepper, and cream. Heat, and taste for seasoning. Serves 8–10.

Sopa de Yautia

SWEET-POTATO SOUP

3 cups diced sweet potatoes
¼ cup minced onions
1½ teaspoons salt
¼ teaspoon white pepper
2 tablespoons minced parsley
4 cups water
2 tablespoons cornstarch
3 cups milk
4 tablespoons butter

Combine the sweet potatoes, onions, salt, pepper, parsley, and water in a saucepan. Bring to a boil and cook over low heat for 30 minutes. Purée in an electric blender or force through a sieve. Return to saucepan. Mix the cornstarch with a little of the milk and add to the soup, stirring steadily to the boiling point. Add the remaining milk and butter. Cook for 10 minutes. Serves 6–8.

≫ੱ *Sopa de Palta*

CREAM OF AVOCADO SOUP

3 avocados
1½ quarts chicken broth
2 stalks celery
2 sprigs parsley
1 teaspoon salt
Dash of cayenne pepper
⅛ teaspoon nutmeg
3 tablespoons butter
2 egg yolks
½ cup heavy cream

Peel and cube the avocados; combine with the broth, celery, parsley, salt, cayenne pepper, and nutmeg. Cook over low heat for 35 minutes. Stir in the butter. Discard celery and parsley; purée the soup in a blender or force through a sieve.

Beat the egg yolks and cream in a bowl; gradually add the hot soup, stirring steadily to prevent curdling. Return to saucepan and cook over low heat, stirring steadily until thickened, but do not let boil. Taste for seasoning. Serve hot or ice-cold. Serves 6–8.

By any name—cassava, mandioca, manioc, farofa—the Brazilians love this starchy flour. On every family table throughout the country there stands either an open bowl or a shaker of this favorite starch.

Farinha de mandioca, a name much used in Brazil for this starch, has an interesting history. The native Indians of the jungle learned that the wild jungle cassava plant, with its attractive foliage, had poisonous roots. However, someone discovered that roasting the tuberous roots removed the deadly hydrocyanic acid which formed a part of its sticky, milky sap. Grated manioc flour is something like grated cheese in appearance and texture, and, in point of fact, the Brazilians use it much as the Italians use cheese, sprinkling it on almost every dish. In rural Brazil, many people could not exist without manioc, but the more sophisticated city people eat it only on rare occasions, or use it as an ingredient, as in the following soup.

✂ *Sopa de Manioc*

TAPIOCA SOUP

1 pound soup meat
1 beef bone
2½ quarts water
2 onions, quartered
2 carrots, sliced
1 parsnip, sliced
3 sprigs parsley
2 stalks celery
2 teaspoons salt
½ teaspoon freshly ground black pepper
½ cup quick-cooking tapioca
½ cup flaked coconut
½ cup heavy cream

In a saucepan, combine the meat, bone, and water. Bring to a boil; add the onions, carrots, parsnip, parsley, celery, salt, and pepper. Cover loosely and cook over low heat for 2½ hours. Strain; return soup to saucepan and add the tapioca. Cook over low heat for 15 minutes.

Rinse the coconut under cold running water and add to the soup with the cream. Cook for 10 minutes. Taste for seasoning. Serves 8–10.

Potage de Tapioca

TAPIOCA-TOMATO SOUP

2 tablespoons butter
1 pound veal, diced
1 cup chopped onions
6 cups chicken broth
2 stalks celery
2 leeks
3 sprigs parsley
2 tomatoes, diced
¼ pound smoked ham, diced
¼ cup quick-cooking tapioca
¼ teaspoon dried ground chili peppers

Melt the butter in a saucepan; brown the veal and onions in it. Add the broth, celery, leeks, parsley, tomatoes, and ham. Cover and cook over low heat for 1 hour. Discard vegetables; stir in the tapioca and chili peppers. Cook for 20 minutes. Taste for seasoning. Serves 6.

Sopa de Arroz con Crema

CREAM OF RICE SOUP

6 cups chicken broth
1 onion, sliced
1 clove garlic, minced
2 stalks celery
¾ cup raw rice
½ teaspoon saffron
¼ teaspoon white pepper
¼ teaspoon nutmeg
1 teaspoon Spanish paprika
2 egg yolks
1 cup light cream   [over]

Combine the broth, onion, garlic, and celery in a saucepan; cook over low heat for 15 minutes. Discard the onion and celery. Add the rice, saffron, pepper, nutmeg, and paprika. Cover and cook over low heat for 30 minutes.

Beat the egg yolks and cream in a bowl; gradually add the hot soup, stirring steadily to prevent curdling. Heat, but do not let boil. Taste for seasoning. Serve with croutons. Serves 4–6.

Ajiaco

POTATO, PEA, AND AVOCADO SOUP

4 tablespoons butter
1½ cups finely chopped onions
3 cups diced potatoes
3 cups chicken broth
¼ teaspoon dried ground chili peppers
⅛ teaspoon saffron
3 cups milk
1 cup cooked or canned green peas
¼ pound cream cheese
3 eggs
1 avocado, peeled and diced

Melt the butter in a saucepan; sauté the onions until browned. Add the potatoes, broth, chili peppers, and saffron. Bring to a boil and cook over low heat for 20 minutes. Mix in the milk and peas; cook for 10 minutes.

Have the cream cheese at room temperature; beat smooth; then beat in the eggs. Gradually add about 2 cups soup, stirring steadily to prevent curdling. Return to balance of soup, mixing steadily. Heat, but do not let boil. Taste for seasoning. Place a few pieces of avocado in each soup plate and pour the soup over them. Serves 6–8.

Sopa de Frijoles Rojo

RED-BEAN SOUP

2 cups dried kidney beans
2 bay leaves
3 quarts water
4 tablespoons olive oil
1½ cups thinly sliced onions
2 cloves garlic, minced
1 tablespoon salt
1 teaspoon freshly ground black pepper
3 cups diced potatoes
3 tablespoons tomato paste
½ teaspoon ground cumin

Wash the beans, cover with water, and bring to a boil. Let soak for 1 hour. Drain, add the bay leaves and the water. Bring to a boil and cook over low heat for 2 hours.

Heat the oil in a skillet; sauté the onions for 10 minutes. Stir in the garlic for 1 minute. Add to the beans with the salt, pepper, potatoes, tomato paste, and cumin. Cook over low heat for 1 hour. Serves 6–8.

EGGS AND CHEESE

EGGS AND CHEESE

Americans think of eggs almost exclusively as a breakfast dish, but Latins have a passion for them at almost any time. Of course, South Americans seldom eat eggs for breakfast, which explains why eggs find a ready place on their luncheon or dinner menus.

Most of the egg recipes presented in this section may be prepared quickly, making them suitable for everyday breakfasts. However, South American egg dishes are particularly ideal for Sunday breakfast when the family palates yearn for a break from the normal routine. Especially worthy of mention is *Llapingachos*, the famous egg dish of Ecuador, consisting of potato pancakes with poached eggs, and just about guaranteed to convert an ordinary Sunday-morning breakfast into a red-letter event.

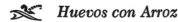 *Ovos Mexidos*

SCRAMBLED EGGS WITH ORANGE JUICE

4 eggs
1 teaspoon salt
½ teaspoon Spanish paprika
¼ cup orange juice
3 tablespoons butter

Beat together lightly the eggs, salt, paprika, and orange juice. Melt the butter in a skillet and scramble the eggs in it over low heat. Serve with buttered toast and orange marmalade. Serves 2.

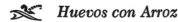 *Huevos con Arroz*

SCRAMBLED EGGS WITH RICE

2 tablespoons olive oil
2 cups chopped green peppers
½ cup chopped onions
1 clove garlic, minced
½ cup raw rice
1 cup boiling water
2 teaspoons salt
½ teaspoon freshly ground black pepper
4 tablespoons butter
6 eggs

Heat the oil in a skillet; sauté the peppers, onions, and garlic for 10 minutes. Stir in the rice; then add the water, salt, and pepper. Cover and cook over low heat for 18 minutes, or until rice is tender. Add the butter. Lightly beat the eggs and stir into the rice mixture until set. Serves 6.

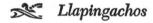 *Huevos Revueltos con Carne*

SCRAMBLED EGGS WITH CHIPPED BEEF

¼ *pound chipped beef*
2 *tablespoons butter*
1½ *cups canned, drained tomatoes*
2 *teaspoons chili powder*
13-ounce *package cream cheese*
6 *eggs*
1 *teaspoon salt*

Shred the beef and cook in the butter for 5 minutes. Add the tomatoes and the chili powder; cook over low heat for 20 minutes. Mash the cream cheese and add, stirring until smooth. Cook for 10 minutes. Beat the eggs and salt and stir into the beef mixture until set. Serves 6.

Llapingachos

ECUADORIAN POTATO PANCAKES
WITH POACHED EGGS

2 *pounds potatoes or* 3 *envelopes instant mashed potatoes*
5 *tablespoons butter*
2 *tablespoons cream cheese*
2½ *teaspoons salt*
½ *teaspoon white pepper*
2 *tablespoons olive oil*
¾ *cup chopped onions*
1 *cup chopped tomatoes*
⅛ *teaspoon dried ground chili peppers*

Cook the potatoes, drain, and mash, or prepare instant mashed potatoes as the package directs. Beat in 2 tablespoons butter, the cream cheese, 1½ teaspoons salt, and the white pepper. Form into flat cakes.

[*over*]

Heat the oil in a saucepan; sauté the onions for 5 minutes. Add the tomatoes, chili peppers, and the rest of the salt. Cook over low heat for 15 minutes.

Melt the remaining butter in a skillet; brown the potato cakes in it. Put some sauce on each pancake and serve with a poached egg on top. Serves 4–6.

Ecuador, as its name implies, lies directly on the equator. It should not, however, be assumed that the entire country lies sweltering in tropical heat. Along the coastline, of course, the climate is hot and humid most of the year; here is where the tropical fruits for which the country is renowned are grown. High up in the rocky Andes (or Cordilleras, as they are called in Ecuador), the weather is springlike all year round, with mild temperatures during the day. At night the air is frequently chilly, often nippy, and, in fact, anything but tropical. Huevos al Horno are just right for a breakfast, lunch, or supper in the United States, too.

Huevos al Horno

BAKED EGGS

6 Uneeda biscuits
¼ cup olive oil
½ cup chopped onions
¾ cup chopped green peppers
1½ cups canned tomatoes
1½ teaspoons salt
½ teaspoon freshly ground black pepper
2 hard-cooked eggs, chopped
6 eggs
1 tablespoon minced parsley

Roll the crackers into crumbs. Heat the oil in a skillet; sauté the onions and green peppers for 5 minutes. Add the tomatoes, salt, and pepper. Cook over low heat for 10 minutes. Stir in the chopped eggs and cracker crumbs; then carefully break the eggs into the sauce. Sprinkle with the parsley. Bake in a 350° oven for 8 minutes or until eggs are set. If you prefer, divide the sauce among individual baking dishes before adding the eggs. Serves 3–6.

Huevos con Salsa de Tomate

DEVILED EGGS IN TOMATO SAUCE

3 tablespoons olive oil
½ cup chopped onions
2 cups canned tomatoes
2 teaspoons cider vinegar
¼ teaspoon chili peppers
2 teaspoons salt
8 hard-cooked eggs
3 tablespoons grated onions
3 tablespoons melted butter

Heat the oil in a saucepan; sauté the onions for 10 minutes. Add the tomatoes, vinegar, chili peppers, and 1½ teaspoons salt. Bring to a boil and cook over low heat for 30 minutes. Taste for seasoning.

Cut the eggs in half lengthwise. Scoop out the yolks and mash with the grated onions, butter, and remaining salt. Stuff the whites and arrange in a baking dish. Pour the sauce over the eggs and bake in a 300° oven for 10 minutes. Serve on rice as a luncheon dish. Serves 4.

Ovos con chorizos

EGGS WITH SAUSAGE

¼ *pound sausage meat or sausages*
2 *tablespoons olive oil*
¼ *cup chopped onions*
4 *eggs*
2 *tablespoons minced parsley*
½ *teaspoon salt*

If sausages are used, remove the meat from casings. Heat the oil in a skillet; sauté the onions for 5 minutes. Mix in the sausage meat; cook until browned. Beat the eggs, parsley, and salt. Pour over the sausages and cook, stirring steadily until set. Serve on toast. Serves 2–4.

Huevos Fritos

PEPPERY FRIED EGGS

1 *tablespoon olive oil*
¾ *cup chopped onions*
⅛ *teaspoon dried ground chili peppers*
1 *cup chopped tomatoes*
1 *teaspoon salt*
2 *tablespoons minced parsley*
3 *tablespoons butter*
6 *eggs*

Heat the oil in a saucepan; sauté the onions for 5 minutes. Add the chili peppers, tomatoes, salt, and parsley; cook over low heat for 5 minutes.

Melt the butter in a skillet; carefully break the eggs into it. Cover and cook over low heat until eggs are firmly set. Serve with the sauce on top. Serves 3–6.

✕ *Huevos Revueltos*

SCRAMBLED EGGS AND GREEN PEPPERS

2 tablespoons olive oil
½ cup chopped onions
1 cup chopped green peppers
¼ cup water
6 eggs
1¼ teaspoons salt
¼ teaspoon white pepper
2 tablespoons butter

Heat the oil in a saucepan; sauté the onions and green peppers for 5 minutes. Add the water and cook over very low heat until absorbed. Cool for 5 minutes.

Beat the eggs, salt, and pepper; stir in the vegetables. Melt the butter in a skillet; scramble the eggs in it. Serves 3–5.

✕ *Huasvulcli*

EGGS, TOMATOES, AND CHEESE

Eggs prepared in this fashion are served during Holy Week in Mexico.

3 tablespoons butter
2 cups peeled chopped tomatoes
1¼ teaspoons salt
2 teaspoons chili powder
4 eggs
4 tablespoons grated Parmesan cheese

Melt the butter in a skillet; cook the tomatoes in it for 10 minutes. Stir in the salt and chili powder. Break the eggs into the skillet and immediately stir gently to break them up. Add the cheese, stirring until set. Serves 3–4.

🐟 *Tortilla de Arroz*

PUFFY RICE OMELET

6 egg yolks
1 teaspoon salt
Dash Tabasco
1 cup cooked rice
6 egg whites, stiffly beaten
2 tablespoons butter

Beat the egg yolks, salt, and Tabasco; stir in the rice. Fold in the egg whites.

Melt the butter in a 9-inch skillet. Pour the mixture into it and bake in a 375° oven for 15 minutes. Serve at once. Serves 3–6.

🐟 *Envueltos de Huevos*

ROLLED OMELET

2 tablespoons olive oil
¾ cup chopped onions
¾ cup chopped green peppers
1¼ cup chopped tomatoes
¼ teaspoon freshly ground black pepper
1½ teaspoons salt
6 eggs
2 tablespoons cold water
2 tablespoons butter
½ cup grated Parmesan cheese

Heat the oil in a saucepan; sauté the onions and green peppers for 10 minutes. Add the tomatoes, pepper, and 1 teaspoon salt; cook over very low heat for 30 minutes.

Beat the eggs, water and remaining salt together. Melt the butter in a 9-inch skillet. Pour the eggs into it and cook, lifting the edges to allow the uncooked portion to run underneath. Sprinkle with the cheese and roll up; turn out onto a heated serving dish and pour sauce over it. Serves 3.

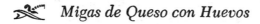 *Migas de Queso con Huevos*

CHEESE-BREAD SAUCE WITH EGGS

8 slices white bread, trimmed
Boiling water
1 cup thinly sliced onions
2 tablespoons butter
2 tomatoes, diced
½ pound cream cheese
¼ teaspoon dried ground chili peppers
½ teaspoon Spanish paprika
1 teaspoon salt
¼ cup chopped green olives
6 poached eggs on toast

Soak the bread in the water; squeeze dry and mash. Sauté the onions in the butter for 10 minutes. Add the tomatoes; cook for 5 minutes. Mix in the cream cheese, bread, chili peppers, paprika, and salt until smooth. Cook for 5 minutes. Stir in the olives. Pour over the eggs. Serves 3–6.

 *Chili con Queso*

CHEESE WITH CHILI

2 tablespoons olive oil
1 cup chopped onions
2 cups drained canned tomatoes
1 teaspoon salt
1 tablespoon chili powder
2 cups grated Cheddar cheese
4 eggs, beaten

Heat the oil in a saucepan and sauté the onions for 10 minutes. Add the tomatoes, salt and chili powder; cook over low heat 30 minutes. Mix in the cheese until melted, then the eggs until set. Serve on toast. Serves 6–8.

Ajoqueso

RAREBIT

3 tablespoons butter
2 green peppers, chopped
½ cup chopped onions
1 clove garlic, minced, or ¼ teaspoon garlic powder
2 cups grated American cheese
1 cup beer
⅛ teaspoon Tabasco

Melt the butter in a saucepan; sauté the peppers, onions, and garlic for 10 minutes. Chop to a paste. Return to the saucepan and mix in the cheese until melted. Gradually add the beer and Tabasco, stirring steadily until smooth. Serve on *tortillas* or toast. Serves 4.

FISH

FISH

The long continent of South America has only two countries without a coastline: Bolivia and Paraguay. With thousands of miles of ocean coast, it is only natural to find that seafood is important in the cuisine of every country. Even in Paraguay and Bolivia, skills in fish cookery are important, for in those countries, river and lake fish are substituted for the ocean fish of their neighbors. You'll enjoy delicious trout from icy Lake Titicaca, as served aboard Panagra flights in South America.

In our own country, admittedly, the preparation of seafood is not too exciting—fish is inevitably fried, occasionally baked or broiled, and that almost completes the scope of native American fish cookery. In South America, on the contrary, great imagination has gone into the preparation of fish, in order to enhance the natural sea flavors; the result is an entire repertoire of unusual and fascinating fish dishes. Interestingly, the style changes from country to country along the varied coast, and the many different national cookery styles are illustrated in these tantalizing recipes. *Caldos* and *guisados* are fish, fish and shellfish, or fish and vegetable stews popular in all Spanish-speaking countries of South America. *Seviche* (or *Cebiche*, as it is sometimes spelled) is a lime- or lemon-marinated raw fish. Don't let this alarm you—remember, clams and oysters are completely raw! And of course for Brazil there is the exotic thick shrimp-and-coconut stew, *Vatapá*.

57

Guisado de Pescado

MIXED SEAFOOD STEW

1½ cups dry white wine
3 cups bottled clam juice
¼ cup grated onions
1 tablespoon minced parsley
1 pound raw shrimp, shelled and deveined
½ pound scallops, quartered
½ pound crab meat
½ teaspoon white pepper
10 oysters, coarsely chopped
2 tablespoons butter

Combine the wine, clam juice, onions, and parsley in a saucepan; bring to a boil and cook over low heat for 10 minutes. Cut the shrimp in quarters and add, with the scallops, crab meat, and pepper. Cook over low heat for 10 minutes. Mix in the oysters and butter; cook for 3 minutes. Taste for seasoning and serve in deep plates. Serves 6–8.

Caldillo de Pescado

FISH SOUP-STEW

½ cup olive oil
1½ cups chopped onions
2 cloves garlic, minced
6 cups water
3 pounds snapper, halibut, or other white-meat fish
2 teaspoons salt
½ teaspoon white pepper
½ teaspoon marjoram
2 cups diced potatoes
½ cup dry sherry
2 cups peeled, diced tomatoes
2 egg yolks
3 tablespoons minced parsley

Heat the oil in a saucepan; sauté the onions and garlic until transparent and lightly browned. Add the water; bring to a boil. Cut the fish in bite-size pieces and add to the saucepan with the salt, pepper, and marjoram. Cover and cook over low heat for 30 minutes. Add the potatoes and sherry; re-cover and cook for 20 minutes. Mix in the tomatoes; cook 10 minutes longer.

Beat the egg yolks in a bowl; gradually add about 2 cups soup, beating steadily to prevent curdling. Return to the saucepan with the parsley, mixing steadily. Heat, but do not let boil. Taste for seasoning. Serves 6–8.

 Pescado en Fuente

FISH CASSEROLE

2½ *teaspoons salt*
½ *teaspoon freshly ground black pepper*
3 *fillets of sole*
3 *tablespoons olive oil*
3 *large onions, sliced*
2 *cups cooked, sliced potatoes*
3 *tomatoes, sliced*
3 *hard-cooked eggs, sliced*
½ *cup bottled clam juice*
3 *tablespoons dry bread crumbs*
2 *tablespoons butter*

Sprinkle half the salt and pepper on the fish; cut in half crosswise. Lightly brown the fish in the oil; remove. Brown the onions in the remaining oil. In a buttered casserole, arrange successive layers of the fish, onions, potatoes, tomatoes, and eggs, sprinkling each layer with a little salt and pepper. Add the clam juice, sprinkle with the bread crumbs, and dot with the butter. Bake in a 375° oven for 50 minutes. Serves 6.

Seviche Chileño

MARINATED FISH, CHILEAN STYLE

1 cup peeled, finely chopped tomatoes
1 cup chopped onions
1 cup lemon juice
½ cup orange juice
1 teaspoon Tabasco
1½ teaspoons salt
⅛ teaspoon dried ground chili peppers
2 pounds raw fish (halibut, sole, snapper)

Mix together in a bowl (not metal) the tomatoes, onions, lemon juice, orange juice, Tabasco, salt, and chili peppers. Wash the fish and cut in bite-size pieces. Add to the previous mixture, mixing well. Marinate in the refrigerator overnight. Serve cold on lettuce leaves. Serves 8–10 as an appetizer.

Caldo de Pescado

FISH STEW

4 tablespoons olive oil
1½ cups chopped onions
1 clove garlic, minced, or ¼ teaspoon garlic powder
3 tablespoons flour
1 cup bottled clam juice
5 cups water
½ cup dry white wine
1½ cups peeled, diced tomatoes
2 teaspoons salt
⅛ teaspoon dried ground chili peppers
¼ teaspoon orégano
6 slices red snapper, whitefish, or halibut
2 tablespoons minced parsley

Heat the oil in a saucepan; sauté the onions and garlic for 5 minutes. Blend in the flour; gradually add the clam juice, stirring steadily to the boiling point. Add the water, wine, tomatoes, salt, chili peppers, and orégano. Cook over medium heat for 30 minutes. Add the fish and parsley; cover and cook over low heat for 30 minutes. Taste for seasoning. Serve in deep bowls with garlic toast. Serves 6–8.

 Cazuela de Pescado

FISH, POTATO, AND RICE CASSEROLE

2 pounds fillet of fish
½ cup olive oil
2 cups thinly sliced onions
3 cups thinly sliced potatoes
2½ teaspoons salt
¾ teaspoon freshly ground black pepper
⅓ cup raw rice
2 tomatoes, sliced
1 cup bottled clam juice
½ cup dry white wine
1 cup water

Cut the fish in bite-size pieces. Pour 2 tablespoons of the oil into a casserole. Spread half the onions on the bottom with half the potatoes over them. Arrange the fish on top of these; sprinkle with half the salt and pepper. Cover with the remaining onions, then the remaining potatoes, the rice and tomatoes. Sprinkle with the remaining salt and pepper. Add the clam juice, wine, and water. Cover and bake in a 350° oven for 1 hour, removing the cover for the last 10 minutes. Serves 6–8.

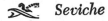 Seviche

MARINATED FISH

6 fillets of snapper, sole, or other white-meat fish
1 cup dry white wine
1 cup lime or lemon juice
2 teaspoons salt
1½ cups thinly sliced onions
1 cup water
½ cup cider vinegar
½ teaspoon dried ground chili peppers

Wash the fillets, remove any bones, and cut in julienne strips. Marinate in the wine, lime or lemon juice, and 1 teaspoon salt for 3 hours.

Soak the onions in the water and remaining salt for 20 minutes. Drain well and squeeze between the hands. Rinse under cold running water and drain again. Soak the onions in the vinegar for 1 hour. Drain well and add to the fish with the chili peppers. Chill for 4 hours. Drain and serve on lettuce. Serves 8–10 as an appetizer.

Along the west coast of South America, near Chile and Peru, flows the Humboldt Current (also called the Peruvian Current) which flows in a northerly direction. It is believed that this strong flow of water is caused by the action of the steady westerly winds upon the great expanse of the South Pacific Ocean, forcing a strong current of icy water to move northward from the cold seas of Tierra del Fuego. This current may be said to resemble our own Gulf Stream, except that our current is warm, whereas the Humboldt Current is cold. As it moves northward, the Humboldt Current draws with it the small fish upon which larger fish of the Pacific feed. For this reason, deep-sea game fishermen fish the Humboldt Current, knowing that its waters conceal large numbers of game fish.

Pescado en Escabeche

FRIED PICKLED FISH

6 *fillets of red snapper, pompano, or sole*
3 *tablespoons lime or lemon juice*
½ *cup sifted flour*
3 *teaspoons salt*
1 *teaspoon freshly ground black pepper*
1½ *cups olive or salad oil*
2 *cups cider vinegar*
½ *cup water*
1 *tablespoon sugar*
2 *cups thinly sliced onions*
2 *cups julienne-cut red or green peppers*
3 *tablespoons capers*
2 *tablespoons mustard pickles*

Cut the fillets in half crosswise and rub with the lime juice; let stand for 10 minutes. Mix together the flour, 2 teaspoons salt, and ¾ teaspoon pepper. Coat the fillets with the mixture. Heat ½ cup oil in a skillet; fry the fish in it until browned on both sides.

In a saucepan, combine the vinegar, water, sugar, onions, peppers, and the remaining salt, pepper, and oil. Bring to a boil and cook over low heat for 5 minutes. Mix in the capers and pickles; pour over the fish and marinate at least 24 hours before serving. Garnish with black olives and cubes of cream cheese, if you wish. Serves 6 as a main course, 12 as an appetizer.

Chile faces along the Pacific Ocean for her entire (and considerable) length. There are many fish and shellfish which are unique or at their best in this country: locos, a sort of cross between abalone and scallops; jaibas, crabs, and amazingly good; chorros, giant clams, ideal for soups and stews. Erizos are sea urchins and have an extraordinary tang of the sea; also, there's luche, the edible seaweed.

Guisado de Pescado

FISH AND VEGETABLE CASSEROLE

1 cup diced potatoes
1½ cups diced tomatoes
1 cup canned corn kernels
1½ cups chopped onions
¾ cup chopped green peppers
6 slices bacon, cut julienne
3 teaspoons salt
¾ teaspoon freshly ground black pepper
¼ cup flour
4 fillets of sole, cut in half
2 tablespoons olive oil

Mix together the potatoes, tomatoes, corn, onions, green peppers, bacon, 1 teaspoon salt, and ½ teaspoon pepper. Combine the flour with the remaining salt and pepper. Dip the fish in the mixture. Heat the oil in a deep skillet or casserole; lightly brown the fish in it. Cover with the vegetables and bake in a 375° oven for 45 minutes. Serves 4–6.

Peruvian history is extremely interesting, possibly the most fascinating of any South American country. The earliest records of a higher order of civilization begin with the Incas, who are believed to have originated at Tiahuanaco, in what is now Bolivia. Incidentally, the word "Inca" refers to the entire race; the Inca is the ruler.

About the year 1100, the Incas first became a nation, with their headquarters in the lofty town of Cuzco, a mountain capital. Over the centuries that followed, their conquests led them north into Ecuador and Colombia and southward toward Chile. In their own way, they greatly resembled the ancient Romans, who conquered almost all of Europe. The civilization that developed was of a surprisingly high type, with a royal family, a state religion, a distinct line of nobility, and a strongly controlled military system. Peculiarly, for such an intelligent race, they never learned to write, but kept accurate records of numerical matters (population, supplies, etc.) *by means of knotted cords called* quipus.

History and the Western world caught up with the Incas at the beginning of the sixteenth century. At that time, the empire was divided between two sons of the deceased monarch—Atahualpa (his favorite) and Huascar (the next in line for succession). The empire was in a turmoil, when in 1532 the Spanish freebooter and conquistador Pizarro arrived at the precise strategic moment. With a small band of soldiers, Pizarro, by means of violence, intrigue, and trickery, conquered the entire empire having a population more than ten thousand times greater than the Spanish force. Atahualpa murdered Huascar; the Spanish captured Atahualpa and demanded an unbelievable ransom for his release—gold to fill an entire room. When the ransom was forthcoming from the ruler's devoted subjects, the Spaniards treacherously murdered Atahualpa.

Life, at least for the rulers and nobility of the ancient Incas, was surprisingly luxurious. Runners brought fresh fish from the ocean over hundreds of miles to the Inca's table, each tiring runner being superseded by another. When the weather was warm, other runners brought snow from the mountaintops to cool the monarch and ice his drinks.

 Seviche Peruano

MARINATED FISH, PERUVIAN STYLE

2 pounds fillet of red snapper, pompano, or sole
½ cup lime or lemon juice
½ cup peeled, chopped tomatoes
½ cup finely chopped green peppers
1 pimiento, chopped fine
¾ cup finely chopped onions
1 clove garlic, minced
1 tablespoon minced parsley
1 teaspoon salt
⅛ teaspoon dried ground chili peppers
1 teaspoon sugar
¼ cup cider vinegar

[over]

Use very fresh fish (frozen fish cannot be substituted). Cut the fillets in finger-length strips; pour the lime or lemon juice over it and turn fish to coat completely. Place in the refrigerator for at least 8 hours. Drain well.

Mix together the tomatoes, green peppers, pimiento, onions, garlic, parsley, salt, chili peppers, sugar, and vinegar. Spread over the fish. Serves 6–8.

Langosta Criolla

LOBSTER IN TOMATO SAUCE

⅔ *cup olive oil*
1 cup chopped onions
2 cups drained canned tomatoes
2 cloves garlic, minced
1½ teaspoons salt
½ teaspoon freshly ground black pepper
2 1½-pound live lobsters
3 tablespoons cognac
2 tablespoons minced parsley

Heat half the oil in a saucepan; sauté the onions for 10 minutes. Add the tomatoes, garlic, salt, and pepper. Cover and cook over low heat for 30 minutes.

The lobster may be prepared in the shell, in which case have them chopped up. Or have the lobsters split, remove the meat, and cut up. Heat the remaining oil in a skillet; cook the lobster in it until shells turn red, or cook the meat for 5 minutes. Heat the cognac, pour over the lobster, and set aflame. When flames die, add to the sauce. Cook over low heat for 15 minutes. Mix in the parsley and taste for seasoning. Serves 2–3.

Brazilian grocery stores are familiarly known as *sêcos e mol-hados*—that is, drys and wets. Many of the ingredients for *Vatapá* are temptingly displayed there. But our local supermarkets are good substitutes, so try *Vatapá* today.

 *Vatapá*

BRAZILIAN SHRIMP-COCONUT STEW

1 cup flaked coconut
2 cups milk
2 tablespoons olive oil
1½ cups finely chopped onions
2 cloves garlic, minced
½ teaspoon dried ground chili peppers
4 cups water
2 teaspoons salt
2 bay leaves
1 pound snapper, halibut, etc., cut in 3-inch pieces
1½ pounds raw shrimp, shelled and deveined
½ pound dried shrimp, finely chopped
2 cups ground peanuts
½ cup yellow corn meal
3 tablespoons butter

Rinse the coconut under cold running water, if the dried variety is used. Combine the coconut and milk; bring to a boil and let soak for 30 minutes. Strain, squeezing out all the milk. Set aside.

Heat the oil in a saucepan; sauté the onions, garlic, and chili peppers for 10 minutes. Add the water, salt, and bay leaves. Bring to a boil; add the fish and raw shrimp. Cook over low heat for 10 minutes. Remove the fish and shrimp; strain the stock. Combine the coconut milk with the dried shrimp and peanuts. Bring to a boil and cook over low heat for 15 minutes. Strain. [over]

Combine the reserved stock with the peanut mixture; bring to a boil, and stir in the corn meal. Cook over low heat for 25 minutes, stirring frequently. Stir in the butter and return the fish and shrimp. Taste for seasoning. Serve in deep bowls. Serves 6–8.

The Brazilians like two drinks which are extremely interesting, with novel flavors: there's the pinga, *made of* pinga *brandy, with lime juice, sugar, and ice added. Also worthy of note is the* batida, *made with white rum and the juice of the* marajuca, *a fruit found only alongside the seashore.*

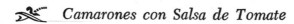 Camarones con Salsa de Tomate

SHRIMP IN TOMATO SAUCE

3 tablespoons olive oil
1 cup thinly sliced onions
1 cup julienne-cut green peppers
2 cups chopped canned tomatoes
1 clove garlic, minced, or ¼ teaspoon garlic powder
1½ teaspoons salt
⅛ teaspoon cayenne pepper
2 pounds raw shrimp, shelled and deveined
¼ cup flour
2 tablespoons butter

Heat the oil in a saucepan; sauté the onions and green peppers for 5 minutes. Add the tomatoes, garlic, salt, and cayenne pepper. Cover and cook over low heat for 25 minutes.

Wash and dry the shrimp; toss with the flour. Melt the butter in a skillet; sauté the shrimp until lightly browned. Add to the sauce; cook over low heat for 5 minutes. Taste for seasoning. Serve with rice. Serves 6–8.

Camarones Saltados

SAUTÉED SHRIMP

3 tablespoons olive oil
½ cup chopped onions
2 pounds raw shrimp, shelled and cleaned
1 clove garlic, minced, or ¼ teaspoon garlic powder
1½ teaspoons salt
¼ teaspoon dried ground chili peppers
½ cup dry white wine
1 tablespoon tomato paste
2 tablespoons minced parsley

Heat the oil in a skillet; sauté the onions for 5 minutes. Add the shrimp, garlic, salt, and chili peppers; sauté for 2 minutes. Mix in the wine, tomato paste, and parsley; cook over low heat for 8 minutes. Taste for seasoning. Serves 6–8.

Camarão Fritos

BATTER-FRIED SHRIMP

(As served aboard Panagra flights in South America)

4 tablespoons lemon juice
6 tablespoons olive oil
1½ teaspoons salt
¼ teaspoon freshly ground black pepper
1½ pounds raw shrimp, shelled and deveined
1 cup sifted flour
2 egg yolks, beaten
⅔ cup water
2 egg whites, stiffly beaten
Fat for deep frying
Minced parsley

[over]

Mix together the lemon juice, 4 tablespoons olive oil, 1 teaspoon salt, and the pepper. Marinate the shrimp in the mixture for 1 hour, then drain. While the shrimp are marinating, prepare the batter.

Sift the flour and remaining salt into a bowl. Blend in the egg yolks and water until smooth. Stir in the remaining oil; let stand for 1 hour. Fold in the egg whites. Dip the drained shrimp in the batter. Heat the fat to 370°; fry the shrimp in it until browned. Sprinkle with parsley and serve with lime or lemon wedges. Spear with cocktail picks to serve as a hot hors d'oeuvre, or serve 4–6.

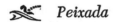 *Peixada*

POACHED FISH AND SHRIMP, BRAZILIAN MANNER

6 slices red snapper or other white-meat fish
2 cups peeled, chopped tomatoes
½ cup sliced scallions (green onions)
2 teaspoons salt
½ teaspoon freshly ground black pepper
1 teaspoon ground coriander
3 tablespoons minced parsley
¾ cup water
1 pound raw shrimp, shelled and deveined

Wash and dry the fish; place in a buttered casserole or deep skillet. Spread the tomatoes, scallions, salt, pepper, coriander, and parsley over the fish. Chill for 3 hours. Add the water, cover, and bring to a boil. Cook over low heat for 30 minutes. Transfer the fish to a serving dish and keep warm. Add the shrimp to the sauce; bring to a boil and cook over low heat for 5 minutes. Taste for seasoning and pour the sauce and shrimp over the fish. Serves 6.

 *Picante de Pescado*

FISH IN ORANGE SAUCE

4 fillets of sole
2 tablespoons coarse salt
¼ cup water
¾ cup orange juice
2 tablespoons lemon juice
½ cup chopped green peppers
1 clove garlic, minced

Cut the fillets in half and rub with the salt. Let stand for 1 hour; rinse under cold running water.

In a deep skillet, combine the water, orange juice, lemon juice, green peppers, and garlic. Place the fish in the skillet. Cover, bring to a boil, and cook over low heat for 20 minutes. Taste for seasoning. Serve cold. Serves 4.

Almejas Fritos

FRIED CLAMS

3 dozen littleneck or cherry-stone clams
1 cup milk
½ cup dry bread crumbs
½ cup flour
Fat for deep frying
¼ pound butter
⅛ teaspoon Tabasco
2 tablespoons minced parsley

Soak the clams in the milk for 10 minutes. Drain well and roll in a mixture of the bread crumbs and flour. Heat the fat to 370° and fry a few clams at a time until browned. Drain.

Melt the butter and stir in the Tabasco and parsley. Pour over the clams or serve in small dishes as a dip. Serves 6–8.

Merluza en Salsa Picante

FISH IN PIQUANT SAUCE

3 tablespoons olive oil
¾ cup minced onions
2 cloves garlic, minced, or ½ teaspoon garlic powder
1 cup chopped tomatoes
½ cup dry white wine
1½ teaspoons salt
¼ teaspoon dried ground chili peppers
2 pounds codfish or halibut
4 tablespoons ground almonds
4 tablespoons heavy cream
2 tablespoons minced parsley

Heat the oil in a deep skillet; sauté the onions until browned. Add the garlic and tomatoes; cook over low heat for 5 minutes. Mix in the wine, salt, and chili peppers. Cut the fish in serving-size pieces and place in the sauce. Cover and cook over low heat for 25 minutes or until fish flakes easily with a fork. Transfer fish to a serving platter. Stir the almonds, cream and parsley into the sauce. Bring to a boil, taste for seasoning, and pour over the fish. Serves 4–6.

It is believed that the Portuguese fishermen crossed the Atlantic to the Grand Banks of Newfoundland centuries before Columbus. Here the intrepid fishermen in their tiny sailboats caught the giant cod found along the underwater slopes of the Grand Banks; because refrigeration was unknown, much of the fish had to be dried by the sun. *Bacalhau*, dried cod, became a staple of the Portuguese daily diet and has so remained throughout the centuries.

When Brazil was first settled by daring Portuguese navigators, they brought with them their familiar *bacalhau*, relying upon it to sustain them when all other fresh foods became tainted. Brazil, of all South American countries, was primarily colonized by the Portuguese and even today has very close diplomatic and emotional ties with Portugal; naturally, the food of Portugal influenced Brazilian cuisine to a large extent. Nothing, however, is more noticeable than the Brazilian fondness for *bacalhau*, the dried codfish which forms the basis of most Brazilian everyday meals. It would certainly be no exaggeration to say that the Brazilians have over fifty different *bacalhau* dishes.

 Bacalhau à Brasileiro

CODFISH CASSEROLE

3 pounds fresh codfish
4 teaspoons salt
¾ teaspoon freshly ground black pepper
6 slices eggplant
⅓ cup olive oil
1½ cups sliced onions
4 tablespoons minced capers
1½ cups drained cooked rice
1½ cups drained canned chopped tomatoes
2 teaspoons Spanish paprika
3 tablespoons butter

Have the codfish cut ½ inch thick and into 6 pieces. Wash and dry; season with 2 teaspoons salt and ½ teaspoon pepper. Sauté the eggplant in half the oil until delicately browned. Arrange on the bottom of a casserole. Sprinkle with 1 teaspoon salt. Sauté the onions in the remaining oil for 10 minutes; spread over the eggplant. Mix the capers and rice; spread over the onions. Arrange the fish on top and cover with the tomatoes. Sprinkle with the paprika and remaining salt and pepper. Dot with the butter. Cover and bake in a 350° oven for 30 minutes. Remove cover and bake 15 minutes longer. Serves 6.

Bacalhau ao Fôrno

BAKED CODFISH

1 pound salt cod
¾ cup olive oil
3 potatoes (1½ pounds), sliced thin
2 cups sliced onions
2 cups chopped tomatoes
½ teaspoon freshly ground black pepper

Soak the codfish in water to cover overnight. Drain, add fresh water to cover, bring to a boil, and cook over low heat for 15 minutes. Let cool in the water. Drain, reserving ¼ cup liquid. Flake the fish.

Heat ¼ cup oil in a skillet; sauté the potatoes until lightly browned. Remove potatoes and sauté the onions until browned. In a casserole, arrange successive layers of the onions, potatoes, fish, and tomatoes, sprinkled with the pepper and remaining oil. Add the reserved liquid. Bake in a 400° oven for 25 minutes. Serves 4–6.

Bacalhau à la Argentina

CODFISH, ARGENTINE STYLE

2 pounds dried codfish
1 onion
1 bay leaf
3 eggs
½ cup olive oil
3 tablespoons lemon juice
⅛ teaspoon dried ground chili peppers
3 tablespoons grated Parmesan cheese
2 tablespoons minced parsley
¾ cup dried bread crumbs
2 tablespoons butter

Wash the codfish and soak in water to cover overnight; change the water twice. Drain, cover with fresh water; add the onion and bay leaf. Bring to a boil and cook over low heat for 30 minutes. Drain and cube. Place in a buttered baking dish. Beat the eggs and gradually add the oil, beating steadily. Stir in the lemon juice, chili peppers, cheese, and parsley. Pour over the fish. Sprinkle with the bread crumbs and dot with the butter. Bake in a 350° oven for 20 minutes, or until browned. Serves 4–6.

 Arroz con Pescado

FISH WITH RICE

4 tablespoons olive oil
1½ cups raw rice
3 cups boiling water
3 teaspoons salt
4 tablespoons butter
1 cup chopped onions
1 clove garlic, minced
3 fillets of sole, cut julienne
½ teaspoon freshly ground black pepper
3 tablespoons minced parsley

Heat 2 tablespoons oil in a saucepan; mix in the rice until yellow. Add the water and 2 teaspoons salt; bring to a boil, cover, and cook over low heat for 15 minutes. Drain, if any water remains.

Heat the butter and remaining oil in a large skillet; sauté the onions and garlic until browned. Add the fish, pepper, and remaining salt; sauté 5 minutes. Lightly mix in the rice and parsley. Cook over low heat for 10 minutes, stirring frequently. Taste for seasoning. Serves 4–6.

≥≈⁻   *Huachinango Asado*

BAKED RED SNAPPER

½ cup olive oil
¾ cup chopped onions
½ cup chopped green peppers
2 cups canned tomatoes
2 cloves garlic, minced, or ¾ teaspoon garlic powder
1 cup dry white wine
⅛ teaspoon dried ground chili peppers
2 bay leaves
3 teaspoons salt
1 4-pound red snapper or other whitemeat fish
½ teaspoon freshly ground black pepper
2 teaspoons Spanish paprika
½ cup chopped stuffed green olives

Heat ⅓ cup oil in a saucepan; sauté the onions and green peppers for 10 minutes. Mix in the tomatoes, garlic, wine, chili peppers, bay leaves, and half the salt. Cook over low heat for 20 minutes.

Wash and dry the fish; rub with the black pepper, paprika, and remaining salt. Heat the remaining oil in a baking dish. Bake the fish in a 450° oven for 10 minutes. Stir the olives into the sauce and pour it over the fish; reduce heat to 375° and bake 35 minutes longer, or until fish flakes easily when tested with a fork. Baste frequently. Serves 6–8.

Pescadilla al Horno

BAKED STUFFED FISH

3 *pounds snapper, whiting, or sea bass*
3 *teaspoons salt*
¾ *teaspoon freshly ground black pepper*
8 *slices white bread*
1 *cup milk*
¼ *cup grated onions*
1 *egg yolk*
¼ *cup minced parsley*
¼ *cup yellow corn meal*
¼ *cup olive oil*
⅓ *cup lemon juice*
¾ *cup sliced onions*
6 *slices lemon*

Have the fish split; season with 2 teaspoons salt and ½ teaspoon pepper. Soak the bread in the milk; drain and mash. Stir in the grated onions, egg yolk, 2 tablespoons parsley, and the remaining salt and pepper. Stuff the fish; sew or skewer the opening. Roll the fish in the corn meal. Heat the oil in a baking dish and place the fish in it. Add the lemon juice, sliced onions, lemon, and remaining parsley. Bake in a 400° oven for 45 minutes, or until fish flakes easily when tested with a fork. Baste frequently. Serves 3–4.

Bollos de Pescado

FISH CROQUETTES

¼ pound butter
3 cups chopped onions
3 pounds mackerel fillets
2 cloves garlic, minced, or ½ teaspoon garlic powder
¼ cup cold water
1 egg, beaten
2 teaspoons salt
¾ teaspoon freshly ground black pepper

Melt half the butter in a skillet; sauté the onions until browned. Grind the fish in a food chopper; then chop with onions until very fine. Mix in the garlic, water, egg, salt, and pepper. Shape into cakes about ¼ inch thick.

Melt the remaining butter in a skillet; sauté the cakes in it over low heat until browned and cooked through. Serve hot or cold. Serves 6–8.

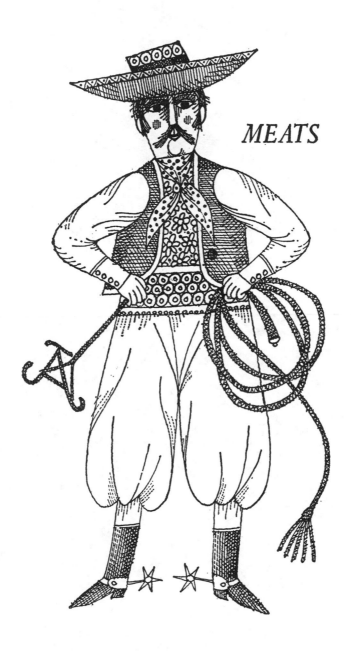

MEATS

MEATS

Argentina, of course, is world-famous for its excellent and inexpensive steaks. Until a few years ago it was customary to serve a broiled steak as a sort of staple food, in addition to whatever main course was ordered, much as we automatically serve potatoes. Although steaks are still quite low in price even today, this delightful custom no longer prevails.

But in South America there is a great variety of excellent, appetizing meat dishes, certainly many more than just plain broiled meats. Delicious sauces are used for basting or marinating the meats to produce fascinating flavors in the finished dishes. *Anticuchos*, Peruvian skewered beef, is a typical example. Fruits and vegetables are frequently cooked together with meats, thus making an all-in-one meal which is simple to prepare. The national stews, combining meats and fruits, or meats and vegetables, make marvelous complete casseroles, perfect for the American housewife and ideal for informal entertaining.

The *Carbonada Criolla* of Uruguay is a delightful dish, incorporating a variety of flavors. In the same way, the *Puchero*, an Argentine boiled dinner, is a sophisticated version of a New England boiled dinner. But what a difference between the two!

All Panagra flights originating in South America serve Argentine meats exclusively, because these are the choicest to be found on the entire continent.

⚓ *Cariucho I*

BRAISED STEAK WITH PEANUT-BUTTER SAUCE

3 pounds round steak
1½ teaspoons salt
½ teaspoon freshly ground black pepper
2 teaspoons Spanish paprika
4 tablespoons olive oil
1 cup chopped onions
½ cup chopped green peppers
1½ cups peeled chopped tomatoes
6 tablespoons peanut butter
2 cups milk, scalded
6 potatoes, cooked and sliced
2 tablespoons minced parsley
2 hard-cooked eggs, chopped

Buy the steak in 1 piece. Season with the salt, pepper, and paprika. Heat 2 tablespoons oil in a casserole; brown the steak in it. Cover and cook over very low heat 1½ hours, or until tender. Add a little water if necessary, to keep from burning.

Prepare the sauce while the steak is cooking. Heat the remaining oil in a skillet; sauté the onions and green peppers for 10 minutes. Add the tomatoes; cook over low heat for 20 minutes. Stir in the peanut butter, and gradually add the milk, stirring steadily until thickened. Taste for seasoning. Cover the steak with the potatoes and pour sauce over all. Sprinkle with the parsley and eggs. Serves 6–8.

⚓ *Cariucho II*

BROILED STEAK WITH PEANUT SAUCE

3 *tablespoons olive oil*
1 *cup chopped onions*
½ *cup chopped green peppers*
1 *cup chopped tomatoes*
1½ *teaspoons salt*
¼ *teaspoon dried ground chili peppers*
1 *teaspoon Spanish paprika*
1 *cup ground peanuts*
1½ *cups chicken broth*
¼ *cup heavy cream*
5 *pounds sirloin steak*

Heat the oil in a skillet; sauté the onions and green peppers for 5 minutes. Add the tomatoes, salt, chili peppers, and paprika; cook over low heat for 5 minutes. Mix in the peanuts and broth; cook for 30 minutes. Stir in the cream; taste for seasoning.

Broil the steak to desired degree of rareness; slice and pour sauce over it. Serve with boiled potatoes. Serves 4–6.

Argentina is truly the granary of the world, supporting untold heads of cattle. The pampas, the vast plains of Argentina, produce in unbelievable abundance crops of wheat, alfalfa, oats, flax, and corn. The cattle are tended by gauchos—that is, cowboys. Although there has been some change recently, it was not too long ago that gauchos went into the pampas with their herds for months at a time; often the cowboys did not see another human being during this entire period. For food, they subsisted almost exclusively upon *maté* (the local tea) and meat. When they grew hungry, the gauchos would kill one of their animals, build a fire, and roast an enormous cut of meat, usually cooked in the animal's hide, *asado con cuero*. On this simple diet of meat and *maté*, they existed for months. The following recipe is a more sophisticated method of meat cookery.

 *Lomito Saltado*

SAUTÉED STEAK AND POTATOES

1 3-pound sirloin steak, cut ½ inch thick
4 tablespoons butter
3 cups peeled, cubed potatoes
4 tablespoons olive oil
1½ cups chopped onions
1½ cups tomatoes
2 teaspoons salt
½ teaspoon dried ground chili peppers
2 tablespoons cider vinegar
1 cup cooked or canned green peas

Cut the steak in strips 1 inch wide by 3 inches long. Melt the butter in a skillet; sauté the potatoes until browned.

Heat the oil in a separate skillet; cook the steak in it over high heat for 3 minutes, shaking the pan frequently. Remove steak and keep warm. In the oil remaining in the skillet, sauté the onions for 5 minutes. Mix in the tomatoes, salt, chili peppers; cook over low heat for 10 minutes. Mix in the vinegar, then the peas, steak, and potatoes. Cook over low heat for 10 minutes, mixing occasionally. Taste for seasoning. Serves 6–8.

⚒️ *Biftec al Horno*

BAKED STEAK

3 pounds round steak
2 teaspoons salt
¼ teaspoon cayenne pepper
½ teaspoon garlic powder
4 tablespoons flour
3 tablespoons olive oil
2½ cups thinly sliced onions
2 teaspoons chili powder
3 tomatoes, sliced
½ cup beef broth

Have the meat cut in 1 piece. Mix together the salt, cayenne pepper, garlic powder, and flour. Rub and pound into the steak. Heat the oil in a skillet; brown the steak on both sides. Transfer to a casserole. Brown the onions in the skillet and spread over the steak. Cover and bake in a 350° oven for 1 hour. Remove cover and add the chili powder and tomatoes. Re-cover and bake for 30 minutes. Add the broth and bake, uncovered, for 20 minutes, or until tender. Serves 6–8.

Did you ever wonder why they call it B.A.? Because its full and correct name is La Ciudad y Puerto de Santa María de los Buenos Aires! That's why. In English it works out as the City and Port of St. Mary of the Good Airs. *Churrasquerias,* steak restaurants with open fires, are very popular here, but other methods of preparation are used too, such as the following steak in batter.

   *Churrasco Rebosado*

BATTER-FRIED FILLET OF BEEF, BUENOS AIRES

4 egg yolks
1¼ cups sifted flour
1½ teaspoons salt
½ teaspoon freshly ground black pepper
1 clove garlic, minced
¼ teaspoon thyme
½ cup milk
4 egg whites, beaten stiff
8 fillets of beef, cut ½ inch thick
1 cup salad oil

Beat the egg yolks until thick and light; mix in the flour, salt, pepper, garlic, and thyme until smooth. Stir in the milk. Fold in the egg whites. Coat the fillets with the mixture.

Heat the oil in a skillet until it bubbles. Fry the fillets 3 minutes on each side or to desired degree of rareness. Serves 8.

   *Bife à la Criolla*

CREOLE BEEF

1 3-pound sirloin steak, ½ inch thick
4 large onions
4 large potatoes
4 tomatoes
⅓ cup olive oil
1 cup chopped green peppers
2½ teaspoons salt
¾ teaspoon freshly ground black pepper
2 cloves garlic, minced, or ½ teaspoon garlic powder
3 tablespoons minced parsley
¾ cup beef broth

Cut the steak in 12 pieces. Slice the onions, potatoes, and tomatoes ¼ inch thick. Heat 2 tablespoons oil in a casserole; arrange successive layers of the steak, onions, potatoes, tomatoes, and green peppers sprinkled with the salt, pepper, garlic, parsley, and remaining olive oil. Add the broth. Bake in a 375° oven for 55 minutes, or until potatoes are tender. Serves 6–8.

Brazil was a part of Portugal until 1822, and the influence of the mother country is still very strong today. Of all the countries of South America, only the Brazilians speak Portuguese, and of all countries, it is the only one to exhibit Portuguese influence in its cooking style.

Another important influence upon the Brazilian food style is that of the Africans, who actually did most of the work of cultivating the country during the past centuries. The earliest cooks were slaves imported from Africa, and to this day the Portuguese and Brazilians say, "A mas preta a cozinheira, o melhor a comida," which translates as, "The darker the cook, the better the food."

Upon awakening, almost everyone drinks a tiny cup of strong black coffee. Later, there is café com leite, *coffee with hot milk, accompanied by crisp rolls and butter plus* marmelada (quince paste). *Lunch and dinner are big meals of many courses. Much of the year brings warm weather, and the local beer is a national favorite. Brazilian beer rates among the world's finest; many Germans came here during the last century and brought with them their brewing methods. Some brands are superb, almost indistinguishable from Pilsner or Munich beer.*

The fruit markets of the country have marvelous produce. In addition to what might be anticipated, there are breadfruit, custard apples, and tamarind, as well as several varie-

[over]

ties without English equivalents—the guaraná, carambola
(each slice in the shape of a five-point star), jaca (about the
size of a watermelon), and dozens of others.

✕ Matambre

STUFFED FLANK STEAK

1 flank steak
2½ teaspoons salt
¾ teaspoon freshly ground black pepper
½ teaspoon thyme
½ cup chopped onions
2 tablespoons minced parsley
¼ cup wine vinegar
4 slices bread
¾ cup milk
1 package frozen chopped spinach, thawed and drained
1 cup cooked or canned green peas
3 hard-cooked eggs, chopped
4 tablespoons grated Cheddar cheese
4 slices bacon, half cooked, drained, and chopped
3 tablespoons olive oil
1 bay leaf

Have the steak pounded thin; rub with the salt, pepper, and
thyme. Place in a bowl and add the onions, parsley, and vinegar.
Marinate in the refrigerator overnight, basting and turning the
meat occasionally.

Soak the bread in the milk; drain and mash smooth. Mix with
the spinach, peas, eggs, cheese, and bacon. Taste for seasoning.
Spread on the drained steak and roll up like a jelly roll. Tie
carefully to keep roll firm. Heat the oil in a casserole or Dutch
oven; lightly brown the meat in it. Add boiling water, to barely
cover the meat, and the bay leaf. Cover and cook over low heat
for 3 hours or until tender. Drain and place a weight on the meat
(a pot cover or board) and chill. Slice thin. Serves 4–6.

⟫ Carne Claveteada

STUFFED STEAK

4 pounds top round
1 cup minced onions
½ cup minced green peppers
1 cup grated carrots
2 teaspoons salt
½ teaspoon freshly ground black pepper
2 tablespoons wine vinegar
2 tablespoons olive oil
2 cups boiling water
½ teaspoon thyme
3 tablespoons minced parsley
1 tablespoon corn meal
½ cup cold water

Have the meat cut in 1 piece. Cut 8 holes in the meat at even intervals. Mix together the onions, green peppers, carrots, salt, and pepper. Stuff the holes with the mixture. Place in a Dutch oven or heavy saucepan; pour the vinegar over the top. Marinate in the refrigerator overnight. Add the oil; cover the pan, and cook over medium heat until meat browns. Add the boiling water, thyme, and parsley. Re-cover and cook over low heat for 2 hours or until tender. Transfer meat to a serving dish and keep warm.

Mix the corn meal and water until smooth; stir into the gravy. Cook over low heat for 10 minutes. Taste for seasoning. Serve gravy in a sauceboat. Serves 6–8.

In Brazil, fresh meat is called carne verde, *or green meat, to distinguish it from dried meat,* carne sêca. *An inexpensive cut of meat becomes a company dish when it's prepared in the Brazilian manner.*

During the seventeenth century, the West Indies and the coasts of South America were harried by pirate raiders. When the French pirates went ashore, they roasted an entire pig or ox, or whatever animal was available, which represented a complete departure from the cooking style of their Gallic homeland. The corsairs called their cooking method *"barbe à queue"*—which means, of course, "beard to tail."

In Haiti, and other West Indian haunts of the pirates the word was shortened to "barbecue." Throughout South America, it is given a Portuguese-Spanish twist and called *"barbacoa."* For the South Americans love to barbecue food, sometimes roasting beef in its own hide, *carne con cuero*, in the Argentine fashion. The gauchos (cowboys) in years gone by would slaughter any animal in sight, just to obtain the meat necessary for one single meal. We use smaller quantities, but their recipes, with excellent results.

 *Lomo Relleno*

ROLLED STUFFED STEAK

3 *pounds round steak, cut ½ inch thick*
½ *pound ground pork*
½ *cup chopped onions*
¼ *cup chopped green peppers*
3 *tablespoons minced pimientos*
2 *tablespoons cider vinegar*
¼ *teaspoon dry mustard*
1 *teaspoon Worcestershire sauce*
3 *teaspoons salt*
¾ *teaspoon freshly ground black pepper*
3 *tablespoons butter*
8 *small white onions*
1 *cup chopped tomatoes*
1 *cup boiling water*

Have the meat pounded as thin as possible. Mix together the pork, onions, green peppers, pimientos, vinegar, mustard, Worcestershire sauce, 1 teaspoon salt, and ¼ teaspoon pepper. Spread on one side of the meat and roll up or fold over. Fasten the edges with skewers or toothpicks, or tie it with string.

Melt the butter in a Dutch oven or heavy saucepan; brown the meat in it. Add the white onions and let brown. Mix in the tomatoes, water, and remaining salt and pepper. Cover and cook over low heat for 2¼ hours, or until tender. Slice and serve with the gravy on top. Serves 6–8.

 *Carbonada*

BEEF-AND-VEGETABLE STEW

4 tablespoons butter
3 pounds cross rib, top sirloin, etc., cut in 1½-inch cubes
1 cup chopped onions
2 teaspoons Spanish paprika
2 cups peeled, cubed potatoes
3 cups boiling water
2 teaspoons salt
½ teaspoon freshly ground black pepper
¼ cup raw rice
½ cup green peas
1 cup diced pumpkin or squash
½ cup corn kernels
2 egg yolks, beaten

Melt the butter in a Dutch oven or heavy saucepan; brown the meat and onions in it. Mix in the paprika and potatoes; let brown for 10 minutes. Add the water, salt, pepper, rice, peas, pumpkin, and corn. Cover and cook over low heat for 1¼ hours, or until tender. Taste for seasoning.

Beat the egg yolks in a deep serving dish; pour the stew over it, mixing lightly. Serves 8–10.

Biftec con Cebollas

STEAK AND ONIONS

¼ pound butter
3 cups finely chopped onions
1½ teaspoons salt
½ teaspoon freshly ground black pepper
4 fillets of beef or individual steaks

Melt all but 2 tablespoons butter in a skillet; sauté the onions over very low heat for 30 minutes, but do not let them brown. Season with the salt and pepper; remove from skillet and keep warm. Melt the remaining butter in the same skillet; cook the steaks in it to desired degree of rareness. Transfer to a serving dish and spoon the onions over them. Serves 4.

Uruguay is a comparatively small country, but one that is extraordinarily progressive. In 1842, before the United States did so (and, incidentally, without bloodshed), slavery was abolished. Uruguay does not have capital punishment; women have had the right to vote for forty years; there are progressive laws covering social security, unemployment, old-age pensions, hours of work, care of the poor and aged, and child welfare; and many other far-reaching efforts to raise the national standard of living are being made. Voting is not only a privilege, but is compulsory; anyone who fails to exercise his right to vote is fined.

Situated between Brazil and Argentina, Uruguay's cuisine contains many meat dishes; and *Carbonada Criolla* is one of the many novel combinations of meat, vegetables, and fruit.

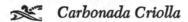 ### Carbonada Criolla

MEAT-AND-FRUIT STEW

3 *tablespoons olive oil*
3 *tablespoons butter*
1½ *pounds beef, cut in ¾-inch cubes*
1½ *pounds veal, cut in ¾-inch cubes*
2 *cups chopped onions*
½ *cup dry white wine*
1 *tablespoon tomato paste*
1 *bay leaf*
2 *teaspoons salt*
½ *teaspoon freshly ground black pepper*
½ *teaspoon thyme*
2 *cups beef broth*
2 *cups cubed potatoes*
2 *cups cubed yellow squash*
2 *cups cubed sweet potatoes*
2 *pears, cubed*
2 *peaches or apples, sliced*
3 *tablespoons seedless raisins*
2 *tablespoons minced parsley*

Heat the oil and butter in a Dutch oven or heavy casserole; brown the beef and veal in it. Remove meat. Brown the onions in the fat remaining in the pan. Return the meat and stir in the wine, tomato paste, bay leaf, salt, pepper, thyme, and broth. Cover and cook over low heat for 1 hour. Add the potatoes, squash, and sweet potatoes; re-cover and cook for 30 minutes. Gently mix in the pears, peaches or apples, and raisins. Cook for 10 minutes. Taste for seasoning, sprinkle with the parsley, and serve with rice. Serves 8–10.

Argentina has three principal cooking styles: Spanish, a natural result of having been settled by Spain; international cuisine, with classic French menus to be found in the best hotels and restaurants; and, most fascinating of all, the *criolla*, or Creole style, based upon campfire cookery, and dating back to Argentina's earliest pioneer days. *Puchero Criollo* is a variation of the Spanish *olla podrida*, potful of good things.

Puchero Criollo

ASSORTED-MEAT DINNER

This recipe was furnished by Panagra's Commissary in Buenos Aires, Argentina.

    1 cup dried chick-peas
    4 quarts water
    2 pounds short ribs of beef
    1 pound pork, cubed
    1 4-pound pullet, disjointed
    3 Spanish or Italian sausages, sliced
    8 small white onions
    8 small carrots
    2 cloves garlic, minced
    2 teaspoons salt
    1 pound yellow squash, peeled and sliced
    4 tomatoes, quartered
    1 2-pound head of cabbage, cut in eighths
    1 cup chopped green peppers
    4 potatoes, peeled and quartered
    6 leeks, cut in half lengthwise
    3 tablespoons minced parsley

Cover the chick-peas with water, bring to a boil, and let soak for 1 hour. Drain. Add the 4 quarts water and bring to a boil.

Add the beef and pork, cover, and cook over medium heat for 1 hour. Add the chicken, sausages, onions, carrots, and garlic; Re-cover and cook over low heat for 45 minutes. Add the salt, squash, tomatoes, cabbage, green peppers, potatoes, and leeks. Re-cover and cook for 45 minutes. Taste for seasoning; mix in the parsley. Arrange the meat and vegetables on a platter. Serve the soup in deep bowls at the same time. Serves 8–10.

 Pimientos Rellenos

STUFFED PEPPERS

8 green peppers
2 tablespoons olive oil
½ cup chopped onions
1 pound ground beef
3 teaspoons salt
¼ teaspoon freshly ground black pepper
2 eggs, beaten
1 cup canned corn kernels
¼ cup chopped green olives
2 cups canned tomato sauce
⅛ teaspoon dried ground chili peppers

Cut a 1-inch piece from the stem end of each of the peppers; scoop out the seeds and fibers. Chop 4 of the tops. Heat the oil in a skillet; sauté the onions and chopped peppers for 5 minutes. Remove from the heat and mix in the beef, 1½ teaspoons salt, the black pepper, and the eggs. Add the corn and olives. Stuff the peppers and arrange in a baking dish. Add the tomato sauce, chili peppers, and remaining salt. Cover and bake in a 350° oven for 1¼ hours, or until peppers are tender. Remove cover for the last 15 minutes of baking time. Serves 4–8.

🐟 Carne Molida Venezolana

VENEZUELAN MEAT LOAF

1 slice white bread
¼ cup milk
½ cup olive oil
2 cups chopped onions
1½ pounds ground beef
2 eggs
¼ cup grated Cheddar cheese
2½ teaspoons salt
¾ teaspoon freshly ground black pepper
¼ cup flour
1 cup peeled chopped tomatoes
¼ teaspoon thyme
3 tablespoons minced parsley

Soak the bread in the milk and mash smooth. Heat half the oil in a skillet; sauté ½ cup onions in it for 10 minutes. Mix with the bread, meat, eggs, cheese, 1½ teaspoons salt, and ¼ teaspoon pepper. Shape into a loaf and sprinkle with the flour.

Heat the remaining oil in a casserole; sauté the remaining onions in it. Add the tomatoes, thyme, parsley, and the remaining salt and pepper. Place the loaf in it. Cover and bake in a 375° oven for 1 hour, basting frequently. Remove cover and bake 10 minutes longer. Serves 6–8.

Locro

BEEF-VEGETABLE STEW

3 tablespoons olive oil
2 pounds beef, cut in 1-inch cubes
¾ cup chopped onions
¾ cup chopped green peppers
3 cups water
1½ cups cubed yellow squash
1½ cups cubed white potatoes
1½ cups cubed sweet potatoes
1 cup corn kernels
1 cup sliced carrots
2½ teaspoons salt
½ teaspoon freshly ground black pepper
2 tablespoons minced parsley

Heat the oil in a casserole or Dutch oven; brown the meat in it. Mix in the onions and green peppers until browned. Add the water, squash, white potatoes, sweet potatoes, corn, carrots, salt, and pepper. Cover and cook over low heat for 2½ hours. The stew should be very thick; add a very little boiling water if necessary. Taste for seasoning and sprinkle with the parsley. Garnish with fried onions and green peppers if desired. Serves 4–6.

⚓ *Albondigón de Chili*

SPICY MEAT LOAF

1 *pound ground beef*
1 *pound ground pork*
¼ *cup minced onions*
¼ *cup minced green peppers*
1 *clove garlic, minced, or* ¼ *teaspoon garlic powder*
1½ *teaspoons salt*
⅛ *teaspoon dried ground chili peppers*
2 *teaspoons chili powder*
2 *eggs*
2 *tablespoons butter*
2 *tablespoons dry bread crumbs*
2 *pimientos, cut julienne*

You may use all beef or all pork if you prefer. Mix together the meat, onions, green peppers, garlic, salt, chili peppers, chili powder, and eggs. Shape into a loaf and place in a baking dish. Dot with the butter and sprinkle with the bread crumbs. Bake in a 400° oven for 1 hour. Decorate with pimientos 5 minutes before the end of baking time. Serve hot or cold. Serves 6–8.

A favorite Brazilian item is *xarque* (which is pronounced *sharkey*) and consists of an air-dried meat. It is prepared from the underpart and sides of beef from which the bones have been removed, soaked in a pickling solution for several days, and then hung out in the hot sun to remove the moisture. Our nearest equivalent is dried chipped beef.

Charquican

CHIPPED BEEF AND VEGETABLES

½ pound chipped beef
3 cups cubed potatoes
1 pound green peas or ½ package frozen
½ pound green beans or ½ package frozen
1 pound yellow squash, cubed
2 cups water
1½ teaspoons salt
2 tablespoons olive oil
½ cup chopped onions
¼ teaspoon dried ground chili peppers
1 tomato, cubed
2 teaspoons paprika
1 cup fresh or canned corn kernels

Soak the chipped beef in cold water for 1 hour. Drain and chop fine. Cook the potatoes, peas, green beans, and squash in the water and salt for 20 minutes. Drain all but ½ cup liquid.

Heat the oil in a saucepan; sauté the onions for 10 minutes. Add the chili peppers, tomato, and paprika. Cook over low heat for 5 minutes. Mix in the corn, beef, and liquid. Cook for 5 minutes, stirring frequently. Combine with the vegetables. Serves 4–6.

Frico

POTATO-MEAT CASSEROLE

2 pounds top sirloin
3 cups sliced raw potatoes
1 cup chopped onions
1 cup chopped green peppers
2 teaspoons salt
2 teaspoons chili powder
¾ cup cracker meal
1 cup chicken broth
1 cup light cream
[over]

Dice the meat small. In a greased casserole, spread some of the potatoes, then some onions and green peppers. Sprinkle with some salt, chili powder, and cracker meal, then make a layer of meat. Repeat until all ingredients are used up, ending with cracker meal. Mix the broth and cream; pour over all. Cover and bake in a 350° oven for 2 hours, removing the cover the last 15 minutes. Serve with a tomato or mushroom sauce. Serves 6–8.

ᴥ *Albondigas con Arroz*

MEAT BALLS WITH RICE

2 tablespoons olive oil
1 cup chopped onions
1 clove garlic, minced
1 pound ground beef
½ cup cooked rice
2 eggs, beaten
2 teaspoons chili powder
3 teaspoons salt
¾ teaspoon pepper
½ cup flour
4 tablespoons butter
1½ cups chopped tomatoes
3 tablespoons minced parsley

Heat the oil in a skillet; sauté the onions for 10 minutes. Mix in the garlic. Cool for 10 minutes. Mix together the onions, meat, rice, eggs, chili powder, 1½ teaspoons salt, and ½ teaspoon pepper. Shape into walnut-sized balls and roll in the flour.

Melt the butter in a skillet; brown the balls in it. Add the tomatoes, parsley, and remaining salt and pepper. Cover and cook over low heat for 30 minutes. Serves 4–6.

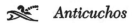 *Anticuchos*

PERUVIAN SKEWERED BARBECUED MEAT

(As served aboard Panagra's flights in Peru)

1 beef heart or 2 pounds sirloin steak
1½ teaspoons salt
½ teaspoon dried ground chili peppers
6 peppercorns
¼ teaspoon saffron
3 cloves garlic, minced
1 cup tarragon vinegar
½ cup water
¼ cup olive oil

Beef heart is used in Peru when preparing *Anticuchos*, but steak is a good substitute. Wash the heart, remove the skin, and cut in 1-inch cubes, or cut the steak in 1-inch cubes. In a bowl, mix the salt, chili peppers, peppercorns, saffron, garlic, vinegar, and water. Marinate the meat in the mixture overnight in the refrigerator.

Drain the meat (reserving the marinade) and thread on 4–6 skewers. Brush with the olive oil. Broil as close to the heat as possible until heart is tender, or steak is at desired degree of rareness. Turn skewers frequently and baste with the marinade. Serves 4–6.

Pastel de Carne Picaday Papas

MEAT PIE WITH POTATO CRUST

¼ cup olive oil
¾ cup chopped onions
1½ pounds ground beef
1½ teaspoons salt
¼ teaspoon dried ground chili peppers
½ cup beef broth
2 tablespoons minced parsley
½ cup seedless raisins
¾ cup sliced green olives
Butter
3 hard-cooked eggs, sliced
1½ cups mashed potatoes or 1 envelope instant mashed
    potatoes
1 egg, beaten

Heat the oil in a skillet; sauté the onions for 5 minutes. Mix in the meat until browned. Add the salt, chili peppers, broth, parsley, raisins, and olives. In a buttered casserole, spread half the meat mixture and arrange the sliced eggs on it. Cover with the remaining meat. Prepare the potatoes as package directs and beat in the egg. Heap over the meat. Bake in a 400° oven for 15 minutes or until browned. Serves 4–6.

 *Trincadillos*

MEAT-AND-RICE CROQUETTES

1 *pound ground beef*
¾ *cup cooked rice*
2 *cups chopped onions*
1½ *teaspoons salt*
½ *teaspoon freshly ground black pepper*
⅛ *teaspoon thyme*
1 *egg, beaten*
3 *tablespoons water*
½ *cup salad oil*

Mix together the beef, rice, onions, salt, pepper, thyme, egg, and water. Shape into 8 croquettes. Heat the oil in a skillet and fry the croquettes until well browned on both sides. Serves 4–6.

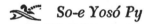 *So-e Yosó Py*

PARAGUAYAN BEEF-AND-RICE HASH

2 *tablespoons olive oil*
¾ *cup chopped onions*
½ *cup chopped green peppers*
1 *pound ground beef*
2 *cups beef broth*
2 *cups cooked rice*
1 *teaspoon salt*
½ *teaspoon freshly ground black pepper*
½ *teaspoon marjoram*
2 *tablespoons minced parsley*

Heat the oil in a skillet; sauté the onions and green peppers for 5 minutes. Mix in the beef until browned. Stir in the broth, rice, salt, pepper, and marjoram. Bring to a boil and cook over low heat for 5 minutes. Taste for seasoning and sprinkle with the parsley. Serves 4–6.

⚒ *Picadillo*

MIXED-MEAT HASH

¼ cup olive oil
1 cup chopped green peppers
1 cup chopped onions
1 clove garlic, minced
1 pound ground beef
½ pound ground pork
1½ teaspoons salt
½ teaspoon freshly ground black pepper
½ cup canned tomato sauce
¼ cup dry white wine
½ cup seedless raisins
¼ cup capers
½ cup sliced almonds

Heat the oil in a large skillet; sauté the green peppers, onions, and garlic for 5 minutes. Add the beef and pork; cook over medium heat, stirring constantly until browned. Mix in the salt, pepper, tomato sauce, wine, and raisins. Cook for low heat for 25 minutes, mixing frequently. Add the capers and almonds; cook 5 minutes longer. Serves 4–6.

In Ecuador the idea of a quick sandwich or a one-course frozen television dinner would make absolutely no headway. A typical family meal throughout the country usually has a minimum of seven or eight courses, and wealthier families usually add a few extra courses, bringing the total up to ten or eleven! If there are guests, or if it is a party or celebration, the sky's the limit. Here is a favorite recipe from Ecuador.

Puerco Horneado

SPICED ROAST PORK

1 6-pound loin of pork
3 cloves garlic, minced
2½ teaspoons salt
1 teaspoon freshly ground black pepper
½ teaspoon saffron
½ teaspoon ground cumin
½ teaspoon marjoram
1 cup boiling water
¼ cup grated onions
2 tablespoons wine vinegar
3 tablespoons minced parsley
½ cup dry white wine
¼ teaspoon dried ground chili peppers

Begin the preparation of the pork the day before it is to be served. Pound to a paste the garlic, salt, pepper, saffron, cumin, and marjoram; rub into the pork. Wrap in waxed paper or foil and refrigerate overnight.

Place pork in a shallow roasting pan. Roast in a 425° oven for 25 minutes. Pour off the fat. Reduce heat to 350°, pour the water over the pork, and roast 2 hours longer, basting frequently. Transfer pork to a platter; skim the fat from the pan and place it over direct heat. Mix in the onions, vinegar, parsley, wine, and chili peppers; bring to a boil, scraping the bottom of the pan. Cook for 2 minutes and serve in a sauceboat. Serves 4–6.

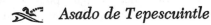 *Corona Asada*

STUFFED CROWN ROAST OF PORK

1 12-rib loin of pork
2 cloves garlic, minced
¾ teaspoon freshly ground black pepper
4 teaspoons salt
3 tablespoons olive oil
1 cup minced onions
½ cup minced green peppers
¾ cup sliced celery
3 tablespoons minced parsley
3 cups cooked rice
½ cup seedless raisins

Have the butcher make a crown of the pork; rub with a mixture of the garlic, pepper, and 3 teaspoons salt. Place in a roasting pan.

Heat the oil in a skillet; sauté the onions, green peppers, and celery for 10 minutes. Mix in the parsley, remaining salt, rice, and raisins. Turn into the crown and cover rice mixture with a piece of aluminum foil. Roast in a 325° oven for 3½ hours, or until tender. Serves 6–8.

Asado de Tepescuintle

MARINATED ROAST PORK

1 8-pound loin of pork
2½ teaspoons salt
1 teaspoon freshly ground black pepper
3 cloves garlic, minced, or ¾ teaspoon garlic powder
½ teaspoon orégano
2 cups chopped onions
2½ cups dry red wine
3 tablespoons olive oil
1½ tablespoons cornstarch

Begin preparation of the dish the day before it is to be served. Rub the pork with a mixture of the salt, pepper, garlic, and orégano. Place in a glass or pottery bowl with the onions and 1½ cups wine. Marinate in the refrigerator overnight, basting frequently.

Heat the oil in a roasting pan. Put the undrained pork into it. Roast in a 350° oven for 3 hours, basting frequently. Pour off the gravy into a saucepan and skim the fat. Mix the cornstarch with the remaining wine and stir into the gravy. Cook over low heat, stirring constantly, until thickened; then cook for 3 minutes longer. Serve with sautéed bananas and rice. Serves 8–10.

 Chiles Rellenos con Puerco

PORK-STUFFED PEPPERS

1½ pounds pork, cubed
1 cup chopped onions
2 cloves garlic, minced
1½ teaspoons salt
¼ teaspoon freshly ground black pepper
1 cup water
3 tablespoons seedless raisins
8 green peppers
1 cup flour
3 egg whites
3 egg yolks
Fat for deep frying

Cook the pork, onions, garlic, salt, pepper, and water over low heat for 30 minutes. Chop or grind the undrained mixture. Soak the raisins in hot water for 10 minutes. Drain and add to the pork mixture.

Wash the peppers; cover with water and bring to a boil; cook over low heat for 10 minutes. Drain, cool, and cut in half lengthwise. Scoop out the seeds and fibers. Stuff the peppers with the

[over]

pork mixture and roll in the flour. Beat the egg whites until stiff, then beat in the egg yolks. Coat the peppers with the eggs.

Heat the fat to 365° and fry 2 peppers at a time until delicately browned. Drain and keep warm while preparing the balance. Serves 8 as a first course or 4 as a main course.

༜ *Lomo de Puerco*

MARINATED PORK STRIPS

½ cup olive oil
3 tablespoons wine vinegar
1½ teaspoons salt
¼ teaspoon dried ground chili peppers
4 tablespoons grated onions
3 cloves garlic, minced or ¾ teaspoon garlic powder
½ teaspoon orégano
2 pork tenderloins (2½ pounds)

Mix together the oil, vinegar, salt, chili peppers, onions, garlic, and orégano. Marinate the pork strips in the mixture 4 hours, turning the meat frequently. Drain, reserving the marinade. Place pork in a shallow roasting pan; roast in a 425° oven for 10 minutes. Pour marinade over the meat; reduce heat to 350° and roast 40 minutes longer, basting frequently. Slice thin. Serves 6–8.

Bolivia is unique among South American countries on several counts. It is the only country without access to the sea; Paraguay has no coastline, but at least it is on the Paraguay River, which runs down to the sea. In Bolivia everything must reach or leave the country via railroad or airplane, for roads are generally unsatisfactory. Part of the country is in the highlands, with extremely rarefied atmosphere, so much so that even walking a few steps is more than the newly arrived visitor can manage. Another portion of Bolivia is subtropical, the Yungas, with hot, humid weather; it is here that tropical fruits are grown. Incidentally, Bolivia was named in honor of Simón Bolívar, the great patriot and revolutionist, who is often called the George Washington of South America.

Here too, stews are served, prepared not only with meat and vegetables but with bananas, nuts, and rice.

Ají de Puerco

BOLIVIAN PORK CASSEROLE

½ cup olive oil
3 cups chopped onions
2 cloves garlic, minced
3 pounds pork, cut in ½-inch cubes
4 tablespoons raw rice
1½ cups chopped tomatoes
2 cups beef broth
2 teaspoons salt
½ teaspoon freshly ground black pepper
¼ teaspoon dried ground chili peppers
¼ teaspoon saffron
4 potatoes, peeled and quartered
3 firm bananas, cut in 2-inch lengths
½ cup ground peanuts
½ cup heavy cream
1 tablespoon molasses

Heat the oil in a casserole; sauté the onions for 5 minutes. Mix in the garlic and pork until browned. Add the rice and tomatoes; cook for 10 minutes. Stir in the broth, salt, pepper, chili peppers, and saffron. Cover and cook over medium heat for 30 minutes. Add the potatoes; cook for 15 minutes. Add the bananas, peanuts, cream, and molasses; cook 15 minutes longer. Taste for seasoning. Serves 6–8.

𝕏 *Lomitos de Chancho*

MARINATED PORK CHOPS

½ *cup wine vinegar*
2 *cloves garlic, minced, or* ½ *teaspoon garlic powder*
½ *teaspoon ground cumin*
¼ *teaspoon dried ground chili peppers*
8 *pork chops, cut* ¼ *inch thick*
1½ *teaspoons salt*
2 *tablespoons olive oil*

Mix together the vinegar, garlic, cumin, and chili peppers. Marinate the chops in the mixture for 1 hour. Drain well. Sprinkle with the salt.

Heat the oil in a skillet; sauté the chops until tender and browned, about 30 minutes. Serves 4.

𝕏 *Puerco con Chili*

PORK CHOPS WITH CHILI

2 *cloves garlic, minced, or* ½ *teaspoon garlic powder*
2 *teaspoons chili powder*
3 *teaspoons salt*
8 *pork chops, cut* ½ *inch thick*
¼ *cup flour*
3 *tablespoons butter*
2 *cups chopped tomatoes*
½ *teaspoon freshly ground black pepper*

Mix together the garlic, chili powder, and 2 teaspoons salt. Rub into the chops, then dust with the flour. Melt the butter in a casserole or deep skillet (with an ovenproof handle). Brown the chops in it. Spread the tomatoes over them and season with the pepper and remaining salt. Cover and bake in a 350° oven for 50 minutes, or until tender. Serves 4.

Pastel de Puerco

PORK PIE

2 tablespoons butter
1½ pounds boneless pork, cut in ¾-inch cubes
½ cup chopped onions
2½ teaspoons salt
½ teaspoon freshly ground black pepper
¾ cup water
1 cup shelled green peas
1 cup corn kernels
½ cup sliced olives
2 cups corn meal
4 cups boiling water
2 eggs, beaten

Melt the butter in a saucepan; brown the pork and onions in it. Add 1½ teaspoons salt, the pepper, and water. Cover and cook over low heat for 45 minutes. Stir in the peas, corn, and olives. Taste for seasoning.

While the pork is cooking, prepare the corn meal. Stir the corn meal and remaining salt into the boiling water. Cook for 20 minutes. Cool 10 minutes; then beat in the eggs. Pour half the mixture into a 1½-quart casserole. Add the pork mixture and cover with remaining corn meal. Bake in a 375° oven for 30 minutes, or until browned. Serves 4–6.

Lomo Negro

PORK IN BLACK SAUCE

8 pork chops, cut ¼ inch thick
3 tablespoons lemon juice
3 tablespoons water
2 tablespoons olive oil
2 teaspoons salt
½ teaspoon freshly ground black pepper
½ cup wine vinegar

[over]

Sprinkle the chops with the lemon juice mixed with the water; let stand for 45 minutes. Heat the oil in a skillet; sauté the chops until very browned. Season with the salt and pepper; add the vinegar. Cover and cook over low heat for 45 minutes, or until tender and very brown. Serves 4.

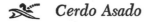 *Cerdo Asado*

ROAST PORK WITH ORANGE GRAVY

1 6-pound loin of pork
¾ teaspoon freshly ground black pepper
3 teaspoons salt
3 cups orange juice
2 tablespoons grated orange rind
2 cloves garlic, minced
¼ teaspoon orégano
1 tablespoon flour
2 cups boiling water

Rub the pork with the pepper and 2 teaspoons salt. Place in a shallow roasting pan; roast in a 375° oven for 30 minutes. Pour off the fat. Mix together the orange juice, rind, garlic, orégano, and remaining salt; pour over the pork. Roast 2 hours longer, basting very frequently. Transfer the pork to a serving platter and skim the fat from the gravy.

Place pan over direct heat and blend in the flour. Add the water, stirring and scraping the bottom of the pan. Cook over low heat for 5 minutes. Carve the pork and pour the gravy over it. Serves 4–6.

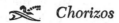 *Chorizos*

PORK SAUSAGES

2 pounds ground pork
½ pound pork fat
1 clove garlic, minced
¾ cup chopped onions
2 teaspoons salt
¾ teaspoon freshly ground black pepper
2 teaspoons Spanish paprika
½ teaspoon dried ground chili peppers
1 teaspoon ground cumin
Sausage casings

Grind all the ingredients together in a food chopper. Fill the sausage casings. Sauté over low heat until browned and cooked through, or use as directed in recipes. If you don't have the casings, form into firm sausage shapes or patties. Makes about 20 sausages.

 Chorizos Revueltos

SCRAMBLED SPICY MEAT

½ pound ground pork
½ pound ground beef
2 tablespoons olive oil
2 cloves garlic, minced, or ½ teaspoon garlic powder
¼ teaspoon dried ground chili peppers
½ teaspoon orégano
1½ teaspoons salt
2 tablespoons water
4 eggs, beaten

[over]

Lightly brown the pork and beef in the oil. Mix in the garlic, chili peppers, orégano, salt, and water. Cook over low heat for 15 minutes, stirring occasionally. Pour the eggs over the mixture and cook, stirring steadily, until set. Serves 4–6.

 Costillas de Cerdo

FRIED, MARINATED SPARERIBS

2 racks spareribs
1 cup cider vinegar
3 tablespoons grated onions
½ teaspoon marjoram
1 teaspoon Spanish paprika
½ teaspoon freshly ground black pepper
2½ teaspoons salt
5 eggs
¼ cup sifted flour
½ cup dry bread crumbs
4 tablespoons minced parsley
Fat for deep frying

Have the spareribs cut into individual ribs. In a bowl, mix the vinegar, onions, marjoram, paprika, pepper, and 1½ teaspoons salt. Marinate the ribs in the mixture for 3 hours at room temperature. Drain and place on a rack in a roasting pan. Roast in a 375° oven for 20 minutes. Cool.

Mix together the eggs, flour, bread crumbs, parsley and remaining salt. Dip the ribs in the mixture, coating them well. Heat the fat to 370°. Fry the ribs in it until browned and crisp. Drain. Serves 4–6. (The ribs are delicious as a hot hors d'oeuvre too.)

☙ *Pecho o Aleta de Ternera*

VEAL ROLL

1 *breast of veal*
3 *teaspoons salt*
½ *teaspoon freshly ground black pepper*
2 *teaspoons paprika*
6 *tablespoons olive oil*
¼ *pound ham, chopped*
3 *eggs*
12 *sour gherkins*
1 *cup chopped onions*
½ *cup grated carrots*
1 *cup chopped tomatoes*
3 *tablespoons minced parsley*
1 *bay leaf*
¼ *teaspoon thyme*
½ *cup dry white wine*
1 *cup sliced stuffed olives*

Have the veal boned and pounded as thin as possible. Season with 2½ teaspoons salt, the pepper and paprika. Heat 2 tablespoons oil in a skillet; sauté the ham for 5 minutes. Make an omelet of the eggs and remaining salt; sprinkle the ham on it and roll up. Place the omelet on the meat and arrange the pickles over it. Roll up the meat and tie with thread.

Heat the remaining oil in a casserole or Dutch oven; brown the meat in it on all sides. Remove, and sauté the onions and carrots until browned. Mix in the tomatoes; cook for 5 minutes. Return the meat and add the parsley, bay leaf, thyme, and wine. Cover and bake in a 350° oven for 2 hours, basting occasionally and adding a little water if necessary. Add the olives and bake 10 minutes longer. Slice and serve. Serves 6–8.

Chuletas de Ternera

VEAL-CHOP CASSEROLE

8 veal chops, ½ inch thick
2 teaspoons salt
½ teaspoon freshly ground black pepper
2 tablespoons olive oil
½ cup chopped mushrooms
¾ cup minced onions
¾ cup dry white wine
½ cup canned tomato sauce
½ square unsweetened chocolate
¼ teaspoon saffron
¼ cup ground almonds

Season the chops with the salt and pepper. Heat the oil in a skillet; brown the chops in it. Transfer to a casserole and cover with the mushrooms. To the oil remaining in the skillet, add the onions. Sauté for 10 minutes. Add the wine and tomato sauce; cook over low heat for 10 minutes. Stir in the chocolate until melted, then the saffron and almonds. Taste for seasoning. Pour over the chops. Cover and bake in a 325° oven for 40 minutes; remove the cover for the last 5 minutes. Serves 8.

Meal hours in Argentina, more so than any other South American country, follow the Spanish custom. Breakfast (taken on arising) is quite simple, coffee and rolls and butter. Lunch, beginning at noon, is a large meal with many courses. Tea is served in the late afternoon, about 5 P.M. or so, and may consist of pastries or sandwiches; but not infrequently it is a substantial meal with meat. The smart time to begin a cocktail party is around nine in the evening, but even as late as 10 P.M. is quite customary. In most restaurants, it's difficult to obtain dinner before 10 P.M. and many smart people wait until eleven or even midnight. But the food is well worth waiting for, particularly when its something like Tongue in Almond Sauce.

Lengua con Almendras

TONGUE IN ALMOND SAUCE, ARGENTINE STYLE

1 5–6-pound pickled tongue
2 tablespoons olive oil
¾ cup chopped onions
2 cloves garlic, minced
¾ cup chopped tomatoes
¼ teaspoon thyme
1 cup ground almonds
½ cup dry bread crumbs
½ cup chopped olives
¼ cup capers

Cook the tongue in boiling water to cover for 3 hours, or until tender. Drain, reserving 2½ cups liquid. Remove the skin and roots of the tongue.

Heat the oil in a saucepan; sauté the onions and garlic for 5 minutes. Add the tomatoes; cook over low heat for 5 minutes. Stir in the thyme, almonds, and reserved liquid. Cook over low heat for 5 minutes. Add the crumbs and olives; cook for 5 minutes.

Slice the tongue and cook in the sauce for 5 minutes. Arrange on a platter and sprinkle with the capers. Serves 8–10.

 Lengua con Hongos

TONGUE IN MUSHROOM SAUCE

1 5-pound smoked tongue
2 cloves garlic, minced
3 tablespoons butter
¾ cup chopped onions
2 cups chopped mushrooms
2 tablespoons flour
1½ cups dry red wine
1 tablespoon minced parsley

[over]

Wash the tongue, cover with water, and bring to a boil. Drain, add fresh boiling water to cover and the garlic. Cover and cook over low heat for 2½ hours, or until tender. Drain, reserving 1½ cups liquid. Remove the skin and roots of the tongue.

Melt the butter in a saucepan; sauté the onions for 5 minutes. Add the mushrooms; sauté for 5 minutes. Stir in the flour until browned. Gradually add the wine and the reserved liquid, stirring steadily to the boiling point. Cook over low heat for 10 minutes. Stir in the parsley. Slice the tongue and serve with the sauce. Serves 8–10.

Tajadas de Lengua Hervida

SLICED TONGUE IN EGG SAUCE

1 5-6-pound pickled tongue
2 tablespoons butter
¼ cup minced onions
1 clove garlic, minced, or ¼ teaspoon garlic powder
¾ cup diced tomatoes
1 bay leaf
2 egg yolks, beaten
¾ cup coarsely chopped walnuts
¼ cup chopped green olives
1 tablespoon capers
1 tablespoon minced parsley

Wash the tongue, cover with water, and bring to a boil. Cover loosely and cook over medium heat for 3 hours, or until tender. Drain, reserving 3 cups stock.

Melt the butter in a saucepan; sauté the onions for 5 minutes. Add the garlic, tomatoes, bay leaf, and reserved stock. Cook over low heat for 20 minutes. Beat the egg yolks in a bowl; gradually add the hot sauce, stirring steadily, to prevent curdling. Return to the saucepan and add the walnuts, olives, capers, and parsley. Heat, but do not let boil. Slice the tongue and pour sauce over it. Serves 8–10.

Riñones al Jerez

KIDNEYS IN SHERRY

3 tablespoons butter
¾ cup chopped onions
1 tablespoon flour
1 cup beef broth
2 tablespoons minced parsley
¼ teaspoon freshly ground black pepper
4 veal kidneys
2 tablespoons olive oil
3 tablespoons dry sherry

Melt the butter in a saucepan; sauté the onions until browned. Sprinkle with the flour, stirring until browned. Add the broth, mixing steadily to the boiling point; cook over low heat for 15 minutes. Mix in the parsley and pepper.

Wash the kidneys and discard the cores. Slice thin. Heat the oil in a skillet; sauté the kidneys over high heat for 1 minute. Add to the sauce with the sherry. Cook over low heat for 5 minutes. Serves 4.

 Guiso de Riñones

SAUTÉED KIDNEYS

6 veal kidneys
3 tablespoons olive oil
1 cup chopped onions
2 teaspoons Spanish paprika
1½ teaspoons salt
¼ cup dry bread crumbs
2 hard-cooked eggs, chopped

[over]

Remove the skin, fat, and core of the kidneys; cube the kidneys. Heat the oil in a skillet; sauté the onions and paprika for 5 minutes. Add the kidneys; sauté for 5 minutes. Sprinkle with the salt and bread crumbs; cook for 1 minute. Garnish with the chopped eggs. Serves 4–6.

 Riñones en Salsa de Tomate

KIDNEYS IN TOMATO SAUCE

3 tablespoons olive oil
1 cup chopped onions
2½ teaspoons salt
1 cup canned tomato sauce
1 cup sliced mushrooms
6 veal kidneys
3 tablespoons butter
2 cups canned small green peas
½ teaspoon freshly ground black pepper
1 tablespoon minced parsley
¼ cup dry white wine
3 hard-cooked eggs, sliced

Heat the oil in a saucepan; sauté the onions for 10 minutes. Add 1½ teaspoons salt, the tomato sauce, and the mushrooms; cook over low heat for 15 minutes.

Remove the skin and fat of the kidneys; discard the core, and slice the kidneys thin. Melt the butter in a skillet; cook the kidneys over high heat for 2 minutes. Add the peas, pepper, parsley, wine, and remaining salt; cook for 1 minute. Combine with the sauce and cook for 2 minutes, or until kidneys are tender. Garnish with the sliced eggs and serve with rice. Serves 6.

Mocoto

CALF'S-FOOT STEW

4 calf's feet
3 quarts water
1 cup sliced onions
3 sprigs parsley
2 stalks celery
1 bay leaf
1 tablespoon salt
½ teaspoon freshly ground black pepper
1 cup chopped tomatoes
½ cup dry red wine
2 egg yolks

Have the feet chopped up into small pieces. Pour boiling water over them, and scrape. Combine the feet with the water, onions, parsley, celery, bay leaf, salt, pepper, and tomatoes. Bring to a boil and cook over low heat for 3 hours. Remove the feet; cut the meat in small pieces, discarding the bones. Add the wine to the stock; cook over high heat for 20 minutes. Return the meat; cook for 10 minutes. Beat the egg yolks in a bowl; gradually add the hot mixture, stirring steadily to prevent curdling. Serve in deep bowls, with garlic toast. Serves 6–8.

Note: You can also make a form of head cheese. Omit the egg yolks. Pour mixture into pie plate and chill until jellied. Serve as an appetizer, cut in wedges.

Coelho Baiana

RABBIT IN ORANGE SAUCE

1 4-pound rabbit, disjointed
¼ cup flour
1½ teaspoons salt
½ teaspoon freshly ground black pepper
2 tablespoons olive oil
¼ pound mushrooms, chopped
1 cup chopped green peppers
1 cup orange juice
2 tablespoons lemon juice
1 tablespoon grated orange rind
½ cup chicken broth

Wash and dry the rabbit. Roll in a mixture of the flour, salt, and pepper. Heat the oil in a casserole or Dutch oven. Brown the rabbit in it. Pour off the fat and add the mushrooms and green peppers; cook for 5 minutes. Add the orange juice, lemon juice, orange rind, and broth. Cover and cook over low heat for 1½ hours, or until tender. Taste for seasoning. Serves 4.

POULTRY

POULTRY

The fine art of cooking poultry in South America consists of far more than merely roasting a fowl, as so many Americans almost automatically do. Easily prepared but intriguingly flavored poultry dishes are the Latin rule, for the routine dish seldom pleases their sophisticated palates. Herbs and spices are used lightly, but with great effect, to flavor delicately the bland meat of poultry. This offers the aspiring cook a wide variety of new and economical specialties, exciting to the taste and far removed from everyday roast chicken or other banalities.

As they say in South America, *"La gallina hace la cocina,"*—"Chicken makes the meal." And to this may be added, turkey and duck too. *Arroz con Pollo,* chicken with rice, can be found in every country of South America, and this is only natural, as it is one of the favorite dishes in Spain.

⚶ Piquete

COLOMBIAN CHICKEN, PORK, AND VEGETABLES

2 cups chopped onions
2 cloves garlic, minced
4 tablespoons minced parsley
½ teaspoon dried ground chili peppers
1 teaspoon ground cumin
3 teaspoons salt
1 5-pound pullet, disjointed
2 tablespoons olive oil
4 cups boiling water
6 pork chops
½ teaspoon freshly ground black pepper
6 white potatoes, peeled and halved
3 sweet potatoes, peeled and halved
4 sweet corn, cut in 2-inch pieces

Begin the preparation the day before the dish is to be served. Pound to a paste the onions, garlic, parsley, chili peppers, cumin, and 2 teaspoons salt. Roll the chicken in the mixture. Cover and chill overnight.

Heat the oil in a saucepan and brown the chicken-and-spice mixture in it. Add the boiling water; cover and cook over low heat for 1¼ hours, or until chicken is tender. Remove chicken, reserving the stock. While the chicken is cooking, season the pork chops with the pepper and remaining salt; sauté until browned and tender.

Add the white and sweet potatoes to the reserved stock. Cook for 15 minutes. Add the corn and cook for 10 minutes. Arrange the chicken and pork on one platter and the vegetables on another.

SERVE WITH THE FOLLOWING SAUCE:

½ *cup cubed white bread*
1 cup milk
¼ *cup olive oil*
1 cup chopped onions
1 teaspoon salt
½ *teaspoon freshly ground black pepper*
1 cup chopped tomatoes
½ *cup grated Parmesan cheese*

Soak the bread in the milk; mash smooth. Heat the oil in a skillet; sauté the onions for 10 minutes. Add the salt, pepper, and tomatoes; cook over low heat for 10 minutes. Mix in the undrained bread; cook over low heat for 3 minutes. Blend in the cheese; cook over low heat for 3 minutes, stirring constantly. Serves 6–8.

 Arroz con Pollo

CHICKEN WITH RICE

1 4-pound pullet, disjointed
3 teaspoons salt
½ *teaspoon freshly ground black pepper*
1 clove garlic, minced
4 tablespoons olive oil
1 cup chopped onions
1½ *cups diced tomatoes*
2 cups raw rice
3 cups hot chicken broth
½ *cup sliced green olives*
½ *cup julienne-cut pimientos*
2 tablespoons minced parsley
1½ *cups canned tiny green peas*

Wash and dry the chicken; rub with 2 teaspoons salt, the pepper and garlic. Heat the oil in a casserole; brown the chicken in it. Stir in the onions until lightly browned. Add the tomatoes;

[*over*]

cover and cook over low heat for 30 minutes. Add the rice and broth and remaining salt; cover and cook over low heat for 30 minutes, or until chicken and rice are tender. Add the olives, pimientos, parsley, and peas; cook 5 minutes longer. Serves 4–6.

ᘔ᠊ᢣ *Gallina à la Colombiana*

CHICKEN IN RICE RING

3 tablespoons olive oil
1 cup minced onions
¾ cup chopped green peppers
2 cloves garlic, minced
1 tablespoon minced parsley
2 3-pound fryers, disjointed
1 cup canned tomato sauce
2 cups dry white wine
1 cup boiling water
2½ teaspoons salt
¼ teaspoon dried ground chili peppers
½ cup seedless raisins
4 cups cooked, drained rice
4 tablespoons melted butter
2 cups grated Cheddar cheese
4 eggs, beaten
1 cup sliced toasted almonds

Heat the oil in a Dutch oven or heavy saucepan; sauté the onions and green peppers for 5 minutes. Add the garlic, parsley, and chicken; sauté for 10 minutes, turning the chicken to coat all sides. Add the tomato sauce, wine, water, salt, and chili peppers. Cover and cook over low heat for 1 hour, or until tender. Cut the chicken from the bones and return to the sauce. Add the raisins; cook over low heat for 15 minutes. Taste for seasoning.

Mix the rice, butter, cheese, and eggs. Pack into a 9-inch buttered ring mold. Bake in a 350° oven for 20 minutes, or until set and browned. Carefully turn out onto a serving dish and fill center with the chicken mixture. Sprinkle the almonds over all. Serves 6–8.

Pollo con Maíz

CHICKEN AND CORN

2 2½-pound fryers, disjointed
2½ teaspoons salt
½ teaspoon freshly ground black pepper
3 tablespoons olive oil
1 cup thinly sliced onions
¾ cup chopped green peppers
2 cloves garlic, minced
1 cup peeled, chopped tomatoes
¾ cup boiling water
3 cups canned corn kernels

Season the chicken with the salt and pepper. Heat the oil in a casserole or Dutch oven; brown the chicken in it. Add the onions and green peppers; let brown. Mix in the garlic, tomatoes, and water. Cover and cook over low heat for 20 minutes. Grind the corn in a food chopper or blender and add to the chicken. Cover and cook for 20 minutes longer, or until tender. Taste for seasoning. Serves 6–8.

Pollo con Frutas

CHICKEN WITH FRUIT

2 3-pound fryers, disjointed
2½ teaspoons salt
½ teaspoon white pepper
4 tablespoons butter
1½ cups chopped canned pineapple
¾ cup seedless raisins
½ cup blanched ground almonds
3 cups orange juice
¼ teaspoon cinnamon
¼ teaspoon mace

[over]

Wash and dry the chicken; season with the salt and pepper. Melt the butter in a Dutch oven or casserole; brown the chicken in it. Add the pineapple, raisins, almonds, orange juice, cinnamon, and mace. Cover and cook over low heat for 1 hour, or until tender. Taste for seasoning. Thicken gravy, if necessary, with a little cornstarch mixed with water. Serve with sliced avocado. Serves 6–8.

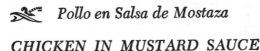 *Pollo en Salsa de Mostaza*

CHICKEN IN MUSTARD SAUCE

2 *3-pound fryers, disjointed*
2½ *teaspoons salt*
½ *teaspoon freshly ground black pepper*
4 *tablespoons butter*
1½ *cups dry white wine*
1 *cup water*
3 *eggs*
3 *tablespoons lemon juice*
1½ *teaspoons dry mustard*
1 *teaspoon sugar*

Wash and dry the chicken; season with the salt and pepper. Melt the butter in a casserole; brown the chicken in it. Add the wine and water; cover and cook over low heat for 45 minutes, or until tender.

Beat the eggs, lemon juice, mustard, and sugar in the top of a double boiler. Place over hot water and cook, stirring steadily, until thickened. Add the gravy from the chicken to the mixture and pour over the chicken. Cook over low heat, basting steadily, until chicken is well coated. Serves 6–8.

Ecuador produces many fruits which are believed to be unique. A trip through any native food market in Ecuador will have displays of numerous fruits completely unknown to the visitor from North America. Of particular interest is the *naranjilla*, an orange with a bright green interior; green orange juice from the *naranjilla* is a taste sensation! The *chirimoya* is another outstanding fruit with a green skin concealing a snowy white interior; it is particularly delicious in ice cream. Our North American orange is a good substitute used in the Eucadorian chicken dish that follows.

 Gallina con Naranjas

CHICKEN WITH ORANGES

1 6-pound roasting chicken, disjointed
2 cups orange juice
1½ cups minced onions
¼ teaspoon dried ground chili peppers
1 bay leaf
4 tablespoons butter
2 teaspoons salt
2 tablespoons flour
½ teaspoon sugar
2 oranges, thinly sliced

Wash and dry the chicken. In a bowl (not metal) mix the orange juice, onions, chili peppers, and bay leaf. Marinate the chicken in the mixture overnight in the refrigerator. Baste frequently.

When ready to cook, drain the chicken, reserving the marinade. Melt the butter in a casserole; brown the chicken in it. Sprinkle with the salt, flour, and sugar, stirring until flour browns. Add the marinade. Cover and cook over low heat for 1½ hours, or until tender. Taste for seasoning. Garnish with the orange slices. Serves 4–6.

Pollo con Garbanzos

CHICKEN WITH CHICK-PEAS

¾ *cup dried or 1½ cups canned chick-peas*
2 *2½-pound fryers, disjointed*
2 *teaspoons salt*
½ *teaspoon freshly ground black pepper*
3 *tablespoons olive oil*
½ *cup chopped onions*
2 *cloves garlic, minced, or ½ teaspoon garlic powder*
2 *tomatoes, diced*
3 *pimientos, cut julienne*

If dried chick-peas are used, cover with water, bring to a boil, and let soak for 1 hour. Drain, cover with fresh water, and cook over medium heat for 1 hour. Drain.

Season the chicken with the salt and pepper. Heat the oil in a casserole or Dutch oven; brown the chicken and onions in it. Add the garlic, tomatoes, and cooked or canned chick-peas. Cover and cook over low heat for 45 minutes, or until chicken and chick-peas are tender, adding a little water if necessary from time to time. Add the pimientos and cook 5 minutes longer. Taste for seasoning. Serves 6–8.

Pollo al Jugo de Uva

CHICKEN IN GRAPE JUICE

2 *pounds seedless green grapes*
2 *2½-pound fryers, disjointed*
2 *teaspoons salt*
¼ *teaspoon white pepper*
4 *tablespoons butter*
2 *tablespoons minced parsley*

Run the grapes in an electric blender until liquid or force through a sieve. Season the chicken with the salt and pepper. Melt the butter in a casserole or Dutch oven; brown the chicken in it. Stir in the parsley, then add the grape juice. Cook over high heat for 10 minutes. Cover and cook over low heat for 45 minutes, or until tender. Serves 6–8.

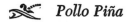 *Pollo Piña*

CHICKEN IN PINEAPPLE SAUCE

2 cups pineapple chunks
½ cup pineapple juice
2 3-pound fryers, disjointed
¼ cup lime or lemon juice
½ cup flour
2 teaspoons salt
½ teaspoon freshly ground black pepper
4 tablespoons butter
½ cup minced onions
¾ cup peeled, chopped tomatoes
2 tablespoons currants or seedless raisins
1 tablespoon brown sugar
3 tablespoons dark rum

Purée the pineapple chunks and juice in a blender, or force through a food mill. Rub the chicken with the lime or lemon juice, then roll in a mixture of the flour, salt, and pepper. Melt the butter in a casserole or Dutch oven and brown the chicken in it. Cover and cook over low heat for 10 minutes. Add the onions and cook for 5 minutes. Mix in the tomatoes, currants or raisins, brown sugar, and pineapple. Cook over low heat for 30 minutes, or until tender. Mix in the rum, taste for seasoning, and serve with rice. Serves 6–8.

Ají de Gallina

PERUVIAN CHICKEN IN SPICY BREAD SAUCE

1 teaspoon dried ground chili peppers
6 slices white bread
2 cups milk
¾ cup olive oil
2 3-pound fryers, disjointed
1 cup chopped onions
1 clove garlic, minced
¾ cup peeled, diced tomatoes
2 cups chicken broth
1½ teaspoons salt
½ teaspoon freshly ground black pepper
4 hard-cooked eggs, sliced
Ripe black olives

Soak the chili peppers in hot water for 15 minutes. Drain. Break up the bread and soak in the milk, then mash very smooth.

Heat the oil in a Dutch oven or heavy saucepan; brown the chicken in it very well. Remove chicken. In the oil remaining, sauté the onions and garlic until browned. Mix in the tomatoes, chili peppers, and mashed bread; cook over high heat for 2 minutes, stirring steadily. Add the broth, salt, and pepper. Bring to a boil and return the chicken. Cover and cook over low heat for 1 hour, or until tender. Serve garnished with the eggs and olives, and with baked sweet potatoes. Serves 8–10.

La Paz (Peace, in English) is the chief city of Bolivia; although the sleepy town of Sucre is the true (constitutional) capital of the country, La Paz is the *de facto* or actual capital. It is a city situated at an altitude of almost two and a half miles, and the thin air requires that the visitor have a day or two of adjustment.

The first day, newcomers will experience difficulty in doing the smallest tasks, such as tying a shoelace or brushing one's teeth. The city is located on a steep plane, and walking about is doubly difficult because of the sharp inclines and the rarefied atmosphere. The Indian market is something not easily forgotten, with most trade being carried on by the womenfolk, who wear colored costumes topped by black derbies. The local markets, with a wide range of foodstuffs on display, is extremely colorful, providing the ingredients for the following dish.

 Pollitos Salteados en Maíz

BOLIVIAN FRIED CHICKEN IN CORN-MEAL BATTER

2 egg yolks
1 cup corn meal
1 cup grated Cheddar cheese
1½ teaspoons salt
½ teaspoon white pepper
2 egg whites, stiffly beaten
2 2½-pound fryers, disjointed
¾ cup salad oil

Beat the egg yolks; stir in the corn meal, cheese, salt, and pepper. Fold in the egg whites. Dip the chicken pieces in the mixture, coating them well.

Heat the oil in skillet and fry the chicken in it until browned and tender. Serves 6–8.

Pollitos Salteados

SAUTÉED CHICKEN

2 2½-pound fryers, disjointed
¼ cup flour
2 teaspoons salt
1 teaspoon Spanish paprika
3 tablespoons olive oil
1 cup chopped onions
¼ teaspoon dried ground chili peppers
2 tablespoons minced parsley
¾ cup dry sherry
½ cup canned tomato sauce
½ cup boiling water

Wash and dry the chicken; roll in a mixture of the flour, salt, and paprika. Heat the oil in a large skillet; brown the onions and chicken in it. Add the chili peppers, parsley, sherry, tomato sauce, and boiling water. Cover and cook over low heat for 30 minutes, or until tender. Taste for seasoning. Serves 6–8.

Pollo Asado

ROAST STUFFED CHICKEN

1 6–7 pound roasting chicken
2½ teaspoons salt
½ teaspoon freshly ground black pepper
1 clove garlic, minced, or ¼ teaspoon garlic powder
2 tablespoons olive oil
½ cup minced onions
1 cup raw rice
2¼ cups hot chicken broth
⅛ teaspoon dried ground chili peppers
2 tablespoons minced parsley
2 tablespoons butter

Season the chicken with the salt, pepper, and garlic. Heat the oil in a saucepan; sauté the onions for 5 minutes. Stir in the rice until coated. Add the broth and chili peppers; cover and cook over low heat for 20 minutes. Mix in the parsley; taste for seasoning and stuff the chicken.

Melt the butter in a roasting pan; place the chicken in it. Roast in a 375° oven for 2¼ hours, or until tender and browned. Serves 4–6.

 *Pollo Relleno*

PORK-STUFFED CHICKEN

1 6–8 pound roasting chicken
3 teaspoons salt
½ teaspoon freshly ground black pepper
2 cloves garlic, minced
1 pound ground pork
½ cup minced onions
1 tomato, chopped
½ cup seedless raisins
½ cup chopped almonds
⅛ teaspoon dried ground chili peppers
3 tablespoons butter

Rub the chicken with a mixture of 2 teaspoons salt, the pepper, and 1 clove garlic. Mix together the pork, onions, tomato, raisins, almonds, chili peppers, and the remaining salt and garlic. Stuff the chicken, closing the opening with skewers or foil. Place in a shallow roasting pan and dot with the butter. Roast in a 350° oven for 2½ hours, or until tender and browned. Baste occasionally with the drippings. Serves 4–6.

In the years of the great rubber boom, a small boom town called Manaus, situated in the midst of the vast Amazon jungle, reached great heights of prosperity. Its leaders and citizens expected a great future for their community: streets were laid out on a grand scale, a vast opera house was built, European opera stars were brought over, and Manaus experienced a great whirl of excitement and land speculation. French chefs served their greatest creations at astronomical prices in quickly built restaurants on the edge of the jungle. In 1913 the worldwide rubber market collapsed, prices fell sharply, and the rapidly built fortunes were as swiftly lost. The restaurants and opera house closed, the chefs and opera stars sadly returned home, and Manaus became a sleepy jungle town once again. But *Canja* is still a popular dish, not only in Manaus, but throughout all of Brazil.

 Canja

CHICKEN AND RICE CREAM

1 5-pound fowl, disjointed
1 tablespoon salt
½ teaspoon freshly ground black pepper
2 tablespoons chicken fat or butter
1 cup sliced onions
1 clove garlic, minced
2 quarts boiling water
1 bay leaf
2 sprigs parsley
⅛ teaspoon marjoram
¾ cup rice

Wash and dry the chicken; rub with the salt and pepper. Heat the fat in a skillet; brown the chicken, onions, and garlic in it. Drain the fat and transfer the chicken and onions to a saucepan.

Add the water, bay leaf, parsley, and marjoram. Cover and cook over low heat for 1 hour. Stir in the rice and cook 2 hours longer. Cut the chicken from the bones and return chicken to soup. Taste for seasoning. Serves 6–8.

 Pastel de Pollo

CHICKEN PIE

1 4-pound pullet, disjointed
2 teaspoons salt
¼ teaspoon dried ground chili peppers
3 tablespoons olive oil
1 cup minced onions
½ cup chopped green peppers
4 tomatoes, diced
1 clove garlic, minced, or ¼ teaspoon garlic powder
2 cups boiling water
¾ cup sliced black olives
2 cups canned corn kernels
Pastry for 1-crust pie

Season the chicken with the salt and chili peppers. Heat the oil in a deep skillet; brown the chicken, onions and peppers in it. Add the tomatoes, garlic and water. Cover and cook over low heat 1 hour, or until tender.

Cut the chicken from the bones and return to the sauce. (If sauce is thin, thicken with a little flour.) Mix in the olives and corn. Taste for seasoning. Turn into a casserole and cover with the pastry. Cut a few slits on top. Bake in a preheated 400° oven for 25 minutes, or until browned. Serves 6–8.

✂ *Pollo al Cazador*

CHICKEN IN RED WINE

½ *cup flour*
2½ *teaspoons salt*
¾ *teaspoon freshly ground black pepper*
2 *3-pound fryers, disjointed*
⅓ *cup olive oil*
8 *small white onions*
1 *cup peeled, chopped tomatoes*
½ *pound mushrooms, sliced*
1 *cup sliced green peppers*
1 *bay leaf*
½ *teaspoon orégano*
1½ *cups dry red wine*
1½ *cups drained canned chick-peas*

Mix together the flour, salt, and pepper; toss the chicken in the mixture. Heat the oil in a casserole or Dutch oven; brown the chicken in it. Add the onions, tomatoes, and mushrooms; cook over medium heat for 10 minutes. Add the green peppers, bay leaf, orégano, wine, and chick-peas. Cover and cook over low heat for 1 hour, or until chicken is tender. Taste for seasoning. Serves 6–8.

In Uruguay, the favorite picnic or outdoor meal dish is undoubtedly pollo asado, *a delicious roast chicken. The Uruguayans, however, have heroic ideas on the subject, often allowing one chicken per person.*

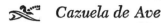 *Cazuela de Ave*

CHICKEN IN THE POT

1 6-pound pullet, disjointed
7 cups water
1 tablespoon salt
½ teaspoon white pepper
1 cup chopped onions
½ cup sliced celery
3 tablespoons butter
2 cups diced potatoes
½ pound green beans, quartered
1 pound green peas, shelled
1 pound yellow squash, sliced
½ cup raw rice
2 hard-cooked eggs, chopped

Combine the chicken, water, salt, pepper, onions, and celery in a saucepan; bring to a boil, cover, and cook over low heat for 1 hour. Remove chicken and drain well. Melt the butter in a skillet; brown the chicken in it.

Add the potatoes, beans, peas, squash, and rice to the stock. Cook over low heat for 30 minutes. Stir in the eggs and return the chicken. Cook for 5 minutes. Serve in deep bowls. Serves 6–8.

ꙮ Ahiaco de Gallina

CHICKEN SOUP-STEW

1 6-pound fowl, disjointed
2½ quarts water
1 onion
2 stalks celery
2 pounds potatoes, sliced
2 tomatoes, sliced thin
8 scallions (green onions), sliced
1 tablespoon salt
½ teaspoon white pepper
½ cup drained capers
2 tablespoons minced parsley

Wash the chicken and combine with the water, onion, and celery. Bring to a boil and cook over low heat for 1¼ hours. Discard the onion and celery; add the potatoes, tomatoes, scallions, salt, and pepper. Cook over low heat for 30 minutes. Remove about half the potatoes and mash them. Return to the saucepan. Taste for seasoning. Just before serving, add the capers and parsley. Serves 4–6.

Rio de Janeiro, the second-largest city in South America, actually means River of January in Portuguese; it was so named, according to reports, because it was discovered during the month of January. Unquestionably the harbor of Rio is the handsomest one in the entire Western Hemisphere. Guanabara Bay, on which Rio fronts, is about ten by twenty miles in size and is surrounded by lofty, imposing mountains. Tourists ride to the top of Sugar Loaf Mountain and Corcovado, both ideal spots for panoramic views of Rio and its fabulous harbor. It has been said that there are three magnificent harbors in the world—Rio, Hong Kong, and Naples. There are many experienced travelers who believe that Rio's is the most impressive of all.

High in the hills surrounding Rio are some excellent restaurants specializing in unusual duck dishes.

 Pato com Môlho de Laranja

DUCK WITH BRAZIL NUTS AND ORANGE SAUCE

1 5-pound duck
6 cups orange juice
1 bay leaf
2 teaspoons salt
½ teaspoon freshly ground black pepper
¼ cup cognac
3 bananas, cut in 2-inch pieces
1 tablespoon cornstarch
¼ cup slivered Brazil nuts
¼ cup curaçao or cointreau

Wash and dry the duck; bring 4 cups orange juice and the bay leaf to a boil in a saucepan. Add the duck; cook over low heat for 1 hour, turning the duck several times. Drain, skim the fat, and reserve 3 cups orange stock. Season the duck with the salt and pepper; place in a shallow roasting pan. Roast in a 450° oven for 20 minutes. Add the remaining orange juice, the cognac, and the bananas. Reduce heat to 350° and roast 45 minutes longer, or until duck is tender. Baste frequently. Transfer the duck and bananas to a serving platter and keep warm. Skim the fat from the pan gravy, and pour the gravy and reserved stock into a saucepan. Mix the cornstarch with a little water to a smooth paste; stir into the gravy until thickened. Add the Brazil nuts and curaçao or cointreau; cook over low heat for 5 minutes.

Carve the duck, pour some gravy over it, and serve the rest in a sauceboat. Serves 4.

Pato en Salsa de Nuences

DUCK IN NUT SAUCE

This recipe was furnished by Panagra's Commissary in Buenos Aires, Argentina.

    2 5-pound ducks, disjointed
    4 cups water
    1 tablespoon salt
    2 tablespoons butter
    ½ cup chopped onions
    1 tablespoon cornstarch
    1 cup ground peanuts
    ⅛ teaspoon dried ground chili peppers
    2 pimientos, cut julienne
    2 tablespoons minced parsley

Remove as much fat as possible from the ducks. Combine in a saucepan with the water. Bring to a boil; add the salt, cover, and cook over low heat for 30 minutes. Remove duck and dry with paper towels. Continue cooking broth until reduced to 2 cups.

Melt the butter in a skillet. Add the duck and onions. Sauté until browned and tender.

Mix the cornstarch with 2 tablespoons cold water; then stir into the broth until thickened. Mix in the peanuts, chili peppers, pimientos, and parsley. Cook over low heat for 5 minutes. Taste for seasoning. Arrange the duck on a platter and pour sauce over it. Serves 6–8.

Pato con Papas

DUCK WITH POTATOES

2 *5-pound ducks, disjointed*
2 *cups thinly sliced onions*
4 *cups boiling water*
2 *cups sliced carrots*
1 *cup sliced celery*
1 *green pepper, cut julienne*
2 *cloves garlic, minced*
1 *tablespoon salt*
1 *teaspoon freshly ground black pepper*
8 *potatoes, peeled and halved*
3 *tablespoons butter*
2 *cups fresh bread crumbs*
3 *hard-cooked eggs, sliced*

Brown the ducks in a saucepan; pour off the fat. Add the onions and brown lightly. Add the water, carrots, celery, green pepper, garlic, salt, and pepper. Bring to a boil, cover, and cook over low heat for 45 minutes. Add the potatoes, re-cover, and cook for 30 minutes. Arrange the duck and vegetables on a platter; keep warm. Reserve 2 cups of the stock.

Melt the butter in a saucepan; mix in the bread crumbs until yellow. Add the reserved stock; cook over low heat for 5 minutes. Taste for seasoning; pour over the duck, and arrange eggs on top. Serves 6–8.

   *Pato com Azeitunas*

DUCK WITH OLIVES

1 5-pound duck, disjointed
2 teaspoons salt
½ teaspoon freshly ground black pepper
2 slices bacon, diced
¾ cup chopped onions
1 cup sliced green peppers
1 clove garlic, minced
1 cup boiling water
1 bay leaf
2 tablespoons minced parsley
24 small stuffed green olives

Wash and dry the duck; remove as much fat as possible. Season with the salt and pepper. Fry the bacon in a Dutch oven or casserole. Add the duck and brown on all sides; pour off the fat. Stir in the onions, green peppers, and garlic until browned. Add the water, bay leaf, and parsley. Cover and cook over low heat for 1¼ hours, or until tender. Skim the fat, taste for seasoning, and add the olives. Cook for 5 minutes. Serves 3–4.

   *Pichones con Guisantes*

SQUABS WITH PEAS

4 squabs or pigeons
4 tablespoons olive oil
3 tablespoons lemon juice
3 tablespoons orange juice
2 teaspoons salt
½ teaspoon freshly ground black pepper
2 tablespoons butter
1 cup dry white wine
1 bay leaf
¼ teaspoon marjoram
2 cups cooked green peas

Wash and dry the whole squabs. Rub inside and out with a mixture of the oil, lemon juice, orange juice, salt, and pepper. Let marinate 4 hours or overnight.

Drain the squabs, reserving any marinade. Melt the butter in a casserole or Dutch oven; brown the squabs in it. Add the marinade, wine, bay leaf, and marjoram. Cover and cook over low heat for 45 minutes, or until tender. Add the peas, taste for seasoning, and cook for 5 minutes. Serves 4.

Chile is a great place for a gourmet who enjoys extremely sophisticated and unusual dishes. At a good restaurant, you'll find such seldom-encountered items as mussels in a rich seafood sauce, pickled wild partridges, grouse prepared with apples and sour cream, wild duck in aspic—not to mention snipe, wild pigeon, and quail. Perhaps best of all is the clawless lobster brought in from Chile's island to the west, San Fernandez, also known as Robinson Crusoe Island. We hope you are fortunate enough to be aboard a Panagra flight when partridge is served—it's absolutely delicious!

Pigeons in red wine are a favorite all through Chile.

 Palomas con Vino Rojo

PIGEONS IN RED WINE

4 pigeons or squabs
2 teaspoons salt
½ teaspoon freshly ground black pepper
3 tablespoons olive oil
¼ cup orange juice
1 tablespoon lemon juice
2 tablespoons butter
¾ cup dry red wine
1 bay leaf
¼ teaspoon marjoram
1 cup sliced, stuffed green olives   [*over*]

Wash and dry the birds; rub inside and out with the salt, pepper, olive oil, orange and lemon juice. Refrigerate overnight.

Melt the butter in a casserole. Brown the drained birds (reserve any liquid) in it. Add the liquid, wine, bay leaf, and marjoram. Cover and cook over low heat for 20 minutes, or until almost tender. Add the olives and cook 10 minutes longer. Taste for seasoning. Serves 4.

 Perú à Brasileira

MARINATED TURKEY

1 8–10-pound turkey
3 cloves garlic, minced
1 tablespoon salt
1 teaspoon freshly ground black pepper
1¼ cups wine vinegar
¾ cup olive oil
2 cups cubed tomatoes
2 cups chopped green peppers
½ cup chopped parsley
1 cup water
¼ pound prosciutto or Parma ham, cut julienne

Begin the preparation of the turkey the night before it is to be served. Rub the turkey with a mixture of the garlic, salt, and pepper. Let it stand for 1 hour. In a deep bowl or pan mix the vinegar, oil, tomatoes, green peppers, and parsley. Marinate the turkey in the mixture in the refrigerator overnight. Baste and turn turkey frequently.

Remove from refrigerator 2 hours before roasting time and baste a number of times. Drain turkey (reserve marinade) and place in a shallow roasting pan. Roast in a 350° oven for 1 hour. Add the marinade and water; roast 1½ hours longer, or until tender. Baste frequently.

Transfer the turkey to a platter; purée the gravy in a blender or force through a sieve. Taste for seasoning; add the ham, and serve in a gravy boat. Serves 8–12.

Pavo Relleno

STUFFED TURKEY

2 cups dry red wine
1 cup minced onions
2 cloves garlic, minced
5 teaspoons salt
1 teaspoon freshly ground black pepper
1 bay leaf
1 12-pound turkey
⅓ cup olive oil
¾ cup chopped green peppers
1½ cups diced onions
½ pound ground pork
2 cups ground almonds
3 hard-cooked eggs
1 cup seedless raisins
½ cup diced prunes
1 cup sliced, stuffed green olives
½ teaspoon thyme
4 slices bread, cubed small

In a bowl (not metal) combine the wine, minced onions, garlic, 3 teaspoons salt, the pepper and bay leaf. Marinate the turkey in the mixture in the refrigerator overnight. Turn turkey frequently and baste.

Heat the oil in a skillet; sauté the green peppers and diced onions for 5 minutes. Stir in the pork until browned and no pink remains. Season with the remaining salt and mix in the almonds, eggs, raisins, prunes, olives, thyme, and bread. Taste for seasoning. Drain the turkey, stuff, and close the openings with skewers or thread. Place in a roasting pan; roast in a 325° oven for 3½ hours, adding the marinade after 1 hour. Baste frequently until turkey is tender. Serves 10–14.

⚡ *Mole de Guajolote*

TURKEY WITH MEXICAN MOLE SAUCE

2 *teaspoons salt*
1 *6–8-pound turkey, cut into serving pieces*
½ *cup olive oil*
1 *slice dry white toast*
2 *tablespoons sesame seeds*
6 *cloves garlic*
3 *green peppers*
8 *tomatoes*
½ *cup almonds*
¼ *teaspoon pepper*
½ *teaspoon cinnamon*
2 *ounces unsweetened chocolate, grated*
2 *tablespoons chili powder*

Combine 1 teaspoon salt and the turkey pieces in water to cover; cook until almost tender, about 1½ hours. Drain carefully, reserving 2 cups of the stock.

Heat ¼ cup olive oil in a skillet. Add the turkey pieces and brown well on all sides. Remove the turkey and place in a casserole.

Grind together the toast, sesame seeds, garlic, green peppers, tomatoes, and almonds. Add the remaining salt, the pepper, cinnamon, chocolate, and chili powder, and mix together well. Heat the remaining oil in the skillet and add the mixture; cook over low heat for 5 minutes, stirring constantly. Place the casserole over low heat and pour the stock over the turkey. Spread the chocolate-spice mixture over the turkey. Cover and cook for 2 hours, stirring occasionally. Serve hot with boiled rice, pouring some of the sauce over the rice. Serves 8.

Cacerola de Pavo

MARINATED TURKEY CASSEROLE

1 8-pound turkey, disjointed
1 tablespoon salt
¾ teaspoon freshly ground black pepper
1 teaspoon paprika
2 cloves garlic, minced
¾ cup wine vinegar
3 tablespoons butter
3 tablespoons olive oil
2 cups chopped onions
2 bay leaves
½ teaspoon ground coriander
1 cup chicken broth
2 cups canned, drained, tiny peas
2 pimientos, cut julienne
1 cup sliced green olives
¼ cup capers

Rub the turkey with a mixture of the salt, pepper, paprika, and garlic. Place in a bowl and pour the vinegar over the turkey. Let marinate for 2 hours at room temperature. Drain.

Heat the butter and oil in a casserole or Dutch oven; brown the turkey and onions in it. Add the bay leaves, coriander, and broth. Cover and cook over low heat for 1½ hours, or until tender. Add the peas, pimientos, olives, and capers; cook for 10 minutes. Taste for seasoning. Serves 6–8.

RICE, CORN, AND BEANS

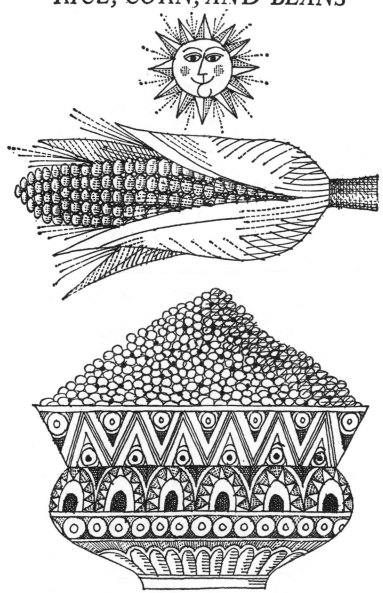

RICE, CORN, AND BEANS 🦃

A Latin meal without beans or rice would be just about unthinkable, very slightly short of sacrilegious. Many South American Indians use beans as the staple of their diet, but the more prosperous people serve beans because they like them as an accompaniment to other dishes. There are scores of different types, sizes, shapes, and flavors of beans, prepared in dozens of different styles, all delightful to the palate, nourishing, and full of vitamins. The Spanish influence on South American cookery fashions is shown in the emphasis on rice preparations; and, of course, in many native dishes, beans and rice are combined to make a very satisfying item.

Corn is served not only on the cob, but in casseroles, stews, breads, desserts, and just about any manner imaginable. In parts of the continent it is a basic, everyday food; in other sections it is rare. The *Sopa de Maíz*, spicy Corn Pudding, is served in place of bread in many countries.

   *Bolinhos de Arroz*

RICE FRITTERS

1 cup rice
2½ cups water
1½ teaspoons salt
1 egg
4 tablespoons minced parsley
3 tablespoons minced onions
¼ cup sifted flour
1 teaspoon baking powder
¼ teaspoon white pepper
Fat for deep frying

Cook the rice in the boiling, salted water for 20 minutes, or until very soft. Drain if any water remains. Purée in an electric blender, or chop fine. Mix in the egg, parsley, onions, flour, baking powder, and pepper.

Heat the fat to 375° and drop the mixture into it by the teaspoon. Fry until browned on all sides. Drain and serve hot, as an accompaniment to meat or poultry. Makes about 30.

    Arroz Verde

GREEN RICE

½ cup olive oil
½ cup chopped green peppers
3 cups cooked rice
¾ cup minced parsley
¾ cup minced spinach
½ cup minced chives
3 eggs
1½ cups light cream
1½ teaspoons salt
¼ teaspoon white pepper
½ cup grated Parmesan cheese

Heat the oil in a skillet; sauté the green peppers for 5 minutes. Mix in the rice, parsley, spinach, and chives. Beat together the eggs, cream, salt, and pepper. Mix into the rice; turn into a buttered 2-quart casserole. Sprinkle with the cheese. Bake in a 350° oven for 35 minutes, or until set and browned. Serves 6–8.

✄ *Arroz con Chorizos*

RICE AND SAUSAGES

4 Spanish or Italian sausages
4 tablespoons olive oil
2 cups rice, washed and drained
½ cup canned tomato sauce
3 tablespoons chopped onions
1 cup canned tiny peas
2 teaspoons salt
½ teaspoon freshly ground black pepper
1 cup water
2 cups hot beef broth
1 tablespoon minced parsley
3 hard-cooked eggs, sliced
1 avocado, peeled and sliced

Remove the skin of the sausages, and slice. Fry until browned; drain.

Heat the oil in a saucepan; sauté the rice until lightly browned. Add the tomato sauce and onions; cook over low heat for 3 minutes. Add the peas, salt, pepper, and water; cook until water is absorbed. Pour in the hot stock; cover and cook for 15 minutes, or until tender and dry.

Sprinkle with the parsley and arrange sausage slices, eggs, and avocado slices over the rice. Serves 4–6.

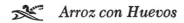 *Camereos*

RICE-AND-SAUSAGE CASSEROLE

1½ cups rice
2 cups water
1½ teaspoons salt
2 tablespoons butter
¾ cup chopped onions
1 clove garlic, minced
3 tomatoes, diced
¼ teaspoon dried ground chili peppers
6 Spanish sausages, sliced

Combine the rice, water, and salt in a saucepan. Cover, bring to a boil, and cook over low heat for 10 minutes. Drain and rinse under cold water; drain again.

Melt the butter in a skillet; sauté the onions for 10 minutes. Mix in the garlic and rice; cook for 2 minutes. Stir in the tomatoes and chili peppers. Turn into a casserole. Brown the sausages in the skillet. Drain, and mix into the rice. Cover and bake in a 350° oven for 30 minutes. Serves 4–6.

Arroz con Huevos

RICE WITH EGGS AND BANANAS

2 tablespoons olive oil
½ cup minced onions
½ pound ground beef
1½ cups raw rice
1½ teaspoons salt
⅛ teaspoon dried ground chili peppers
3½ cups beef broth
6 fried eggs
3 bananas, sliced and sautéed

Heat the oil in a saucepan; sauté the onions for 5 minutes. Mix in the meat until browned. Add the rice, stirring until well coated. Stir in the salt, chili peppers, and broth. Cover and cook over low heat for 25 minutes. Heap into 6 mounds; place an egg on each and surround with bananas. Serves 6.

 Arroz con Carne

RICE-AND-MEAT CASSEROLE

4 tablespoons olive oil
1½ cups chopped onions
1 clove garlic, minced
1 cup sliced green peppers
3 pounds top round, chuck, etc., cut in 1-inch cubes
2½ teaspoons salt
½ teaspoon freshly ground black pepper
½ teaspoon Spanish paprika
3 cups boiling water
½ pound Spanish or Italian sausages, sliced
1 cup raw rice
½ cup sliced stuffed olives
4 tablespoons minced parsley

Heat the oil in a Dutch oven or casserole; sauté the onions, garlic, and green peppers for 10 minutes. Remove. In the oil remaining, brown the meat. Return the sautéed vegetables; add the salt, pepper and paprika, and boiling water. Cover and cook over low heat for 2 hours. Mix in the sausages and rice; re-cover and cook for 30 minutes. Watch carefully to prevent burning. The finished dish should be fairly dry. Toss in the olives and parsley. Taste for seasoning. Serves 8–10.

 *Sopa Seca*

CHICK-PEAS AND RICE

CHICK-PEAS:

> 2 tablespoons olive oil
> 1 cup chopped onions
> 2 cloves garlic, minced
> 1½ pounds ground pork
> 1½ cups chopped tomatoes
> 2 cans chick-peas, drained
> 1½ teaspoons salt
> ¼ teaspoon dried ground chili peppers

Heat the oil in a saucepan; brown the onions in it. Mix in the garlic and pork until browned. Add the tomatoes, chick-peas, salt, and chili peppers. Cover and cook over low heat for 45 minutes. Prepare the rice while the chick-pea mixture is cooking.

RICE:

> ¼ cup olive oil
> 2 cups raw rice
> ½ cup chopped onions
> ½ cup chopped green peppers
> 1 clove garlic, minced
> 2 cups canned tomatoes
> 2 cups boiling water
> 2 teaspoons salt
> ½ teaspoon freshly ground black pepper
> ½ teaspoon orégano
> ½ cup seedless raisins
> ½ cup sliced almonds

Heat the oil in a saucepan; sauté the rice, onions, and green peppers until browned. Mix in the garlic, tomatoes, boiling water, salt, pepper, and orégano. Cover and cook over low heat for 25 minutes. Mix in the raisins and almonds. Combine with the chick-pea mixture. Serves 6–8.

⚞ *Arroz Mexicana*

MEXICAN RICE

4 tablespoons olive oil
1 cup chopped onions
2 cups rice
2 cloves garlic, minced
1 cup chopped green peppers
1 cup chopped tomatoes
1 canned Jalapeño chili, minced, or ¼ teaspoon dried
   ground chili peppers
2 teaspoons salt
2 teaspoons chili powder
3½ cups boiling water
¾ cup sliced stuffed green olives

Heat the oil in a casserole; sauté the onions for 10 minutes. Stir in the rice and garlic until rice turns transparent. Add the green peppers, tomatoes, Jalapeño chili, salt, chili powder, and boiling water. Cover and cook over low heat for 25 minutes, or until rice is tender and dry. Garnish with the olives. Serves 6–8.

Brazil was originally settled by Portuguese explorers, and even today Portuguese is the language of the country, rather than Spanish, which is spoken in almost all the other nations. Like the Portuguese, the Brazilians make frequent use of olive oil, dried codfish, garlic, tomatoes, onions, flavorsome spices, and rice—and around the equator, there is a heavy hand with peppers and various other hot ingredients.

Arroz com Mariscos combines rice with the local variety of clam, resulting in a delightful dish.

Arroz com Mariscos

RICE WITH CLAMS

3 *dozen littleneck or cherry-stone clams or 2 cans minced
    clams*
2 *cups water*
2 *sprigs parsley*
1 *bay leaf*
1 *stalk celery*
3 *tablespoons chopped onions*
½ *teaspoon marjoram*
1½ *cups raw rice*
¾ *cup peeled, chopped tomatoes*

If fresh clams are used, scrub them well with a brush and keep
under running water for 10 minutes. Combine the 2 cups water,
parsley, bay leaf, celery, onions, and marjoram in a large saucepan. Bring to a boil and cook over low heat for 10 minutes.
Discard parsley, bay leaf, and celery. Add the clams; cover and
steam until clams open. Remove clams; discard shells. (If canned
clams are used, drain the clams. Combine juice, and enough
water to measure 2 cups, with the parsley, bay leaf, celery,
onions, and marjoram. Cook 5 minutes and discard parsley, bay
leaf, and celery.) Add rice and tomatoes to the liquid. Cover
and cook over low heat for 18 minutes or until tender. Add a
little boiling water if rice becomes too dry. Drop the steamed
or minced clams in the rice and cook 2 minutes longer. Taste for
seasoning, and add salt if necessary. Serve with Parsley Butterballs scattered on top.

PARSLEY BUTTERBALLS:

4 *tablespoons butter*
2 *tablespoons minced parsley*

Cream together the butter and parsley. Form ½ teaspoons of
the mixture into balls. Serves 4–6.

Pudín de Maíz

CORN-MEAL PUDDING

2 tablespoons olive oil
¾ cup chopped onions
½ cup chopped green peppers
1 pound ground beef
2 teaspoons salt
¼ teaspoon dried ground chili peppers
½ cup seedless raisins
½ cup sliced black olives
4 egg yolks
1½ cups corn kernels
1 teaspoon sugar
4 egg whites, stiffly beaten

Heat the oil in a skillet; sauté the onions and green peppers for 5 minutes. Mix in the meat, 1¼ teaspoons salt, and the chili peppers until browned. Add the raisins and olives. Turn into a greased 1½-quart casserole.

Beat the egg yolks and remaining salt; stir in the corn and sugar. Fold in the egg whites. Heap over the meat mixture. Bake in a preheated 400° oven for 20 minutes, or until puffed and browned. Serves 4–6.

Just as an American might be surprised to find a portion of meat served without potatoes, in the same fashion a Paraguayan would be astonished not to be served corn with any meat dish.

Pastelito de Choclo

MEAT-AND-CORN CASSEROLE

¼ pound butter
1 cup chopped onions
1 cup diced green peppers
1½ cups chopped tomatoes
1½ pounds ground beef
2½ teaspoons salt
½ teaspoon freshly ground black pepper
3 hard-cooked eggs, chopped
½ cup currants or seedless raisins
3 cups corn kernels
¾ cup sifted flour
2 tablespoons sugar
1 cup milk
7 eggs, beaten

Melt half the butter in a skillet; sauté the onions and green peppers for 10 minutes. Mix in the tomatoes, the meat, 1½ teaspoons salt, and the pepper; cook for 10 minutes, stirring frequently. Stir in the eggs and currants; remove from heat.

Grind the corn, or purée in a blender. Melt the remaining butter in a saucepan; blend in the flour, sugar, and remaining salt. Add the milk, mixing until smooth. Stir in the corn; cook over low heat for 10 minutes. Cool for 10 minutes, then beat in the eggs. Turn half the corn mixture into a 2-quart buttered casserole; pour the meat mixture over it, and cover with the remaining corn mixture. Bake in a preheated 350° oven for 35 minutes, or until set and browned. Serves 6–8.

✳ *Flan de Maíz*

CORN CUSTARD

4 eggs
1½ cups milk
1¼ teaspoons salt
⅛ teaspoon white pepper
1½ cups corn kernels
3 tablespoons minced pimientos

Beat the eggs, milk, salt, and pepper. Stir in the corn and pimientos. Pour into a buttered 1½-quart casserole or 6 custard cups. Place in a shallow pan of hot water. Bake in a preheated 300° oven for 1 hour for the large one, 40 minutes for the individual cups, or until a knife inserted in the center comes out clean. Serves 6.

✳ *Pastel de Choclo*

MEAT-CORN PIE

½ cup seedless raisins
3 tablespoons olive oil
1 cup thinly sliced onions
1 pound ground beef
3 teaspoons salt
¼ teaspoon dried ground chili peppers
1 tablespoon flour
3 tablespoons water
¾ cup sliced stuffed olives
½ teaspoon ground cumin
2 tablespoons butter
½ cup chopped onions
2 cups fresh or canned corn kernels

[over]

Soak the raisins in hot water while preparing the meat. Heat the oil in a skillet; sauté the sliced onions for 5 minutes. Mix in the meat until browned. Add 2 teaspoons salt, the chili peppers, and the flour mixed with the water. Cook over low heat for 5 minutes, stirring frequently. Remove from heat and mix in the olives, cumin seed, and drained raisins. Turn into a 10-inch buttered pie plate.

Melt the butter in the skillet; sauté the chopped onions for 5 minutes. Mix in the corn and remaining salt; cook over low heat for 5 minutes, stirring frequently. Spread over the meat. Bake in a 350° oven for 15 minutes. Serves 4–5.

In Colombia there is a favorite Sunday breakfast, and many people eat it fifty-two Sundays a year. It consists of a *tamal* or *humita* and is usually served with hot chocolate, bread, and cheese. American breakfast cereals have made some inroads on local customs, but the *tamal* with hot chocolate is still a national favorite for Sunday morning.

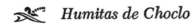 *Humitas de Choclo*

CORN TAMALES

4 cups canned corn kernels
¾ cup minced onions
1 cup chopped tomatoes
1½ teaspoons salt
¼ teaspoon dried ground chili peppers
2 tablespoons minced parsley
2 tablespoons olive oil

Mix all the ingredients together. Cut 12 6-inch squares of aluminum foil and divide the mixture among them in the center of the foil. Roll up and twist ends to seal. Cook in boiling water for 45 minutes. Drain and serve in the foil. If you prefer, turn mixture into a buttered baking dish. Cover and bake in a 375° oven for 25 minutes. Serves 6.

Humitas

SAUTÉED CORN

3 tablespoons butter
½ cup chopped onions
½ cup chopped tomatoes
2½ cups corn kernels
1 teaspoon salt
1 teaspoon sugar
¼ cup milk

Melt the butter in a skillet; sauté the onions for 5 minutes. Mix in the tomatoes; sauté for 5 minutes. Add the corn, salt, sugar, and milk; cook over low heat for 30 minutes, mixing steadily. Serves 3–4.

 Humitas con Leche

BAKED CORN CASSEROLE

6 tablespoons butter
1 cup chopped onions
1 cup chopped green peppers
1 cup chopped tomatoes
4 cups fresh or canned corn kernels
1½ teaspoons salt
¼ teaspoon dried ground chili peppers
2 tablespoons sugar
2 teaspoons paprika
1 cup hot milk
¼ cup dry bread crumbs

Melt 4 tablespoons butter in a casserole; sauté the onions for 10 minutes. Add the green peppers and tomatoes; sauté for 5 minutes. Mix in the corn, salt, chili peppers, sugar, and paprika.

[*over*]

Cook over low heat for 2 minutes. Gradually add the milk, mixing steadily. Sprinkle with the bread crumbs and dot with the remaining butter. Bake in a 375° oven for 15 minutes, or until delicately browned. Serves 6–8.

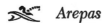 *Pudín de Maíz y Queso*

CORN-CHEESE PUDDING

4 cups corn kernels
4 eggs, beaten
1 cup light cream
1½ teaspoons salt
Dash cayenne pepper
1½ teaspoons paprika
⅓ cup melted butter
6 thin slices Cheddar cheese

Mix together the corn, eggs, cream, salt, cayenne pepper, paprika, and butter. Spread half the mixture on the bottom of a buttered 9-inch pie plate. Arrange the cheese over it and cover with the remaining corn mixture. Bake in a 325° oven for 30 minutes, or until firm. Serves 6–8.

 Arepas

VENEZUELAN CORN CAKES

2¼ cups white corn meal
3½ cups water
1½ teaspoons salt
¼ cup oil

Mix the corn meal with 1 cup cold water. Bring the remaining water and salt to a boil; stir in the corn meal until thickened, then turn off heat, but keep on burner while beating with a wooden spoon. Turn out onto a board until cool enough to handle. Knead until smooth and shiny. Form into 2-inch balls and flatten. Heat some oil in a skillet, bake until lightly browned, add more oil, and turn the cakes.

Place under the broiler and broil until a thick crust is formed (about 20 minutes). Turn cakes every 5 minutes. Split and serve hot with butter. Makes about 18.

Sopa de Maíz

SPICY CORN PUDDING

5 tablespoons butter
¾ cup chopped onions
¾ cup chopped tomatoes
2 teaspoons salt
½ teaspoon freshly ground black pepper
½ cup water
1½ cups corn meal
2 teaspoons baking powder
1 cup grated Cheddar cheese
1 cup milk
3 tablespoons salad oil or beef drippings

Melt the butter in a skillet; sauté the onions for 5 minutes. Add the tomatoes, salt, and pepper; sauté for 5 minutes. Stir in the water; cook over low heat for 5 minutes.

Mix together the corn meal, baking powder, cheese, and milk. Stir in the tomato mixture until smooth. In an 8-inch-square pan, heat the oil until it bubbles; pour the mixture into it. Bake in a preheated 375° oven for 35 minutes, or until browned and set. Cut in squares and serve hot as an accompaniment to meat or poultry. Serves 4–6.

The world's highest airport is located at La Paz, Bolivia. The city is situated at 12,000 feet, but, believe it or not, the airport (called El Alto de la Paz) is at 13,500 feet, about 1500 feet higher than the city! It's a thrilling experience to land or take off from El Alto Airport on your Panagra plane. Not too far away is Lake Titicaca, the world's loftiest navigable lake. The first steamboat to be used on the lake was carried piecemeal by Indian porters from the lowlands and assembled at the lake shore.

Spicy vegetable preparations are a staple of the Bolivian diet.

 Picante de Maíz Boliviano

BAKED-POTATO-AND-CORN CASSEROLE

2 cups fresh or canned corn kernels
½ cup milk
½ cup chopped onions
½ cup chopped green peppers
¼ teaspoon dried ground chili peppers
⅛ teaspoon nutmeg
2 teaspoons salt
4 potatoes (2 pounds) cooked, peeled, and sliced thin
½ teaspoon freshly ground black pepper
¾ cup grated Cheddar cheese
4 hard-cooked eggs, sliced

Purée the corn and milk in an electric blender or put through a food mill. In a saucepan, combine the corn, onions, green peppers, chili peppers, nutmeg, and 1 teaspoon salt. Cook over low heat for 5 minutes, stirring frequently.

In a buttered casserole, arrange layers of the potatoes sprinkled with the pepper and remaining salt, the cheese and eggs. Pour the corn mixture over the top. Bake in a preheated 400° oven for 15 minutes. Serves 6–8.

✂ Pan de Maíz

CORN-BREAD PUDDING

3 tablespoons olive oil
1½ cups chopped onions
1 cup chopped tomatoes
¾ cup beef broth
3 tablespoons butter
2 cups corn meal
1 teaspoon salt
1 teaspoon baking powder
½ pound cottage cheese
1½ cups milk

Heat the oil in a skillet; sauté the onions for 10 minutes. Add the tomatoes; cook over low heat for 10 minutes. Mix in the broth; cook for 10 minutes. Stir in the butter until melted. Cool for 10 minutes.

Sift the corn meal, salt, and baking powder into a bowl. Mix in the cottage cheese, then gradually beat in the milk. Blend in the onion mixture. Turn into an 8-inch-square buttered baking pan. Bake in a preheated 350° oven for 50 minutes, or until set. Cut in squares and serve with meat, poultry, or fish dishes. Serves 4–6.

In Brazil, there's one favorite combination dish served all over the country, a sort of Blue Plate Special. It customarily consists of rice with black beans, a slice or two of beef, a few small pork ribs, three small link sausages, a fried egg, and several fried bananas. You'll never go hungry in Brazil!

How would you like to follow a Brazilian cookbook? A typical measurement might call for "a plateful of flour"! Instead of an exact measurement in the American style, the Brazilian cook dips a dinner plate into a flour bin and then shakes the plate several times to and fro; when the flour is gently rounded, without peaks, it's considered a plateful. But if you think that's indefinite, how about a fistful of flour? That's another common Brazilian cookery measurement.

The Brazilian cook doesn't measure too carefully for *Feijoada,* either, but uses any meat that happens to be available.

 Feijoada Completa

BRAZILIAN BLACK BEANS AND ASSORTED MEATS

1 pound dried beef
3 cups dried black beans
2 pounds corned beef
¼ pound bacon
3 pounds loin of pork
1½ teaspoons salt
½ teaspoon freshly ground black pepper
1 cup orange juice
1 cup dry red wine
3 tablespoons olive oil
1 cup chopped onions
2 cloves garlic, minced
½ pound Spanish sausages, sliced
¼ teaspoon dried ground chili peppers

Soak the dried beef in cold water overnight. Drain, cover with fresh water, and bring to a boil. Cook for 5 minutes. Drain and cut in small pieces.

Wash the beans, cover with water, and bring to a boil; let soak for 1 hour. Drain, add fresh water to cover, and cook over low heat for 2 hours. Cook the meats at the same time. Combine the dried beef, corned beef, and bacon in a saucepan. Add water to cover. Bring to a boil; cover and cook over low heat for 2½ hours. Season the pork with the salt and pepper; roast in a 375° oven for 1¾ hours. Drain the boiling meats and add to the beans. Remove 1 cup beans and purée in an electric blender or mash into a paste. Return to the remaining beans with the orange juice and wine. Cook over low heat for 1 hour.

Heat the oil in a skillet; sauté onions and garlic for 5 minutes. Add the sausages and let brown. Add to the beans with the chili peppers. Cook for 30 minutes.

Slice the boiled meats and roast pork; arrange on a platter. Put the beans in a deep bowl. Serve with rice, sliced oranges, and pickled onions. White rum is the customary drink served with *Feijoada*. Serves 10–12.

🐟 *Frijoles à la Yucateca*

BEANS AND PORK, YUCATÁN STYLE

3 *cups black beans*
4 *teaspoons salt*
6 *pork chops, cut ¼ inch thick*
¼ *teaspoon freshly ground black pepper*
2 *cups boiling water*
½ *cup olive oil*
2 *cups chopped onions*
2 *cloves garlic, minced*
½ *teaspoon dried ground chili peppers*
1 *onion, thinly sliced*
½ *cup grated Cheddar cheese*

[over]

Wash the beans. Cover with water and bring to a boil. Let soak for 1 hour; drain, add fresh water to cover, and bring to a boil. Cook over low heat for 2 hours, or until tender. Add 3 teaspoons salt after 1 hour. Drain if any liquid remains.

While the beans are cooking, season the chops with the pepper and remaining salt. Brown the chops lightly; add the boiling water. Cover and cook over low heat for 30 minutes. Cut the chops in half.

Heat the oil in a casserole; sauté the chopped onions for 10 minutes. Add the garlic, beans, undrained pork, and the chili peppers. Cover and cook over low heat for 30 minutes. Arrange the onion slices on top and sprinkle with the grated cheese. Serves 6–8.

The Indian natives of Mexico relied chiefly upon the local produce available to them as the basis for their diet. Beans, corn, and chilis were the chief ingredients. The Mayans, those astonishing predecessors of the Mexican Indians, lived almost exclusively upon corn, as historical relics and writings indicate. The nobility ate the finest—game, fresh fish, and other delicacies, but the peasants existed entirely upon corn—as a cereal, in pancakes, and as an alcoholic beverage.

When the Spaniards arrived and conquered Mexico, they brought with them their Spanish cookery style, and the refinement in Mexican cooking dates from that time (roughly, the seventeenth century). It should be emphasized that, even today, the typical peon of Mexico often still eats the simple Mexican food that his forefathers did two and three centuries ago. Later, when Napoleon put Maximilian and Carlota upon the throne of Mexico as emperor and empress, they brought Austrian and Belgian cooking to their court, but the general public disregarded their customs, for the rulers were politically unpopular.

⚗ *Frijoles Refritos*

RE-FRIED BEANS

2 cups dried red beans
1 onion
⅓ cup olive oil
1 clove garlic, minced
2 teaspoons salt
¼ teaspoon dried ground chili peppers

Wash the beans, cover with water, and bring to a boil. Let soak for 1 hour. Drain, add fresh water to cover, and the onion. Bring to a boil and cook over low heat for 2 hours, or until tender. Drain. Purée ¾ cup of the beans in an electric blender, or mash very smooth.

Heat the oil in a skillet; stir in the whole beans, garlic, salt, and chili peppers. Cook over medium heat for 5 minutes, stirring frequently. Mix in the puréed beans. Cook until crisp and dry, mixing almost steadily. Taste for seasoning. Serves 4.

⚗ *Frijoles Negros y Blancos*

BLACK AND WHITE BEANS

2 cups dried black beans
2 cups dried white beans
8 cloves garlic
1 tablespoon salt
½ cup olive oil
1 cup finely chopped onions
2 cloves garlic, minced
6 slices bacon, cooked, drained, and crumbled
1 teaspoon ground cumin
½ teaspoon freshly ground black pepper

[over]

Wash the black and white beans separately; place in separate saucepans. Cover with water, bring to a boil, and let soak for 1 hour. Drain. Add fresh water to cover and 4 cloves garlic to each saucepan. Bring to a boil, cover, and cook over low heat for 2 hours, or until tender. Drain. Combine the beans and salt in a casserole.

Heat the oil in a skillet; sauté the onions for 10 minutes. Stir in the garlic for 1 minute, then add to the beans with the bacon, cumin, and pepper. Mix lightly; cook over low heat for 20 minutes. Taste for seasoning. Serves 6–8.

Lentejas con Tomates

LENTILS IN TOMATO SAUCE

2 cups lentils
4 cups water
2 teaspoons salt
¼ cup olive oil
1 cup chopped onions
2 cloves garlic, minced, or ½ teaspoon garlic powder
1 green pepper, diced
2 cups canned tomato sauce
¼ teaspoon dried ground chili peppers
1 teaspoon chili powder
¼ pound ham, diced small

Wash the lentils; combine with the water and salt. Bring to a boil and cook over low heat for 1½ hours, or until tender. Drain. While the lentils are cooking, prepare the sauce.

Heat the oil in a skillet; sauté the onions, garlic, and green pepper for 10 minutes. Add the tomato sauce, chili peppers, chili powder, and ham. Cook over low heat for 15 minutes. Add the lentils. Taste for seasoning. Turn into a baking dish; bake in a 400° oven for 15 minutes. Serves 6–8.

⚞ *Frijoles Fritos con Queso*

FRIED BEANS WITH CHEESE

2 cups dried red or black beans
1 onion, quartered
6 tablespoons olive oil
3 teaspoons salt
½ teaspoon freshly ground black pepper
2 cups grated Cheddar cheese

Wash the beans, cover with water, and bring to a boil; let soak for 1 hour. Drain, add fresh water to cover, and bring to a boil. Add the onion and 1 tablespoon oil. Cook over low heat for 2 hours, or until tender, adding 2 teaspoons salt after 1 hour of cooking. Drain and mash the beans.

Heat the remaining oil in a skillet; fry the bean paste, pepper, and remaining salt in it until browned and crisp. Sprinkle with the cheese; bake in a 375° oven for 10 minutes, or until cheese melts. Serves 4–6.

⚞ *Lentejas con Chorizos*

LENTILS WITH SAUSAGES

2 cups lentils
3 tablespoons olive oil
¾ cup chopped onions
1 clove garlic, minced
½ cup diced tomatoes
2 teaspoons salt
½ teaspoon freshly ground black pepper
6 Spanish or Italian sausages, sliced
2 pimientos, cut julienne
2 tablespoons minced parsley

[over]

Cook the lentils in boiling water for 45 minutes. Drain. Heat the oil in a saucepan; sauté the onions and garlic for 10 minutes. Add the tomatoes, salt, pepper, and lentils. Cover and cook over low heat for 15 minutes. Brown the sausages, drain, and add with the pimientos and parsley. Cook for 5 minutes. Taste for seasoning. Serves 6–8.

➤❊ *Garbanzos al Horno*

BAKED CHICK-PEAS

1 pound chick-peas
1 bay leaf
2 cloves
½ teaspoon thyme
½ teaspoon freshly ground black pepper
2 teaspoons salt
½ pound salt pork, diced
1 cup chopped onions
1 clove garlic, minced, or ¼ teaspoon garlic powder
1 teaspoon dry mustard
3 tablespoons minced parsley
¼ cup dark corn syrup

Wash the chick-peas, cover with water, and bring to a boil. Remove from the heat and let soak for 1 hour. Drain, cover with fresh water, and bring to a boil. Add the bay leaf, cloves, thyme, and pepper. Cook over medium heat for 1½ hours, adding the salt after 1 hour of cooking time.

Sauté the salt pork and onions together for 5 minutes. Pour off half the fat. In a bean pot or casserole, combine the undrained chick-peas, the onion mixture, the garlic, mustard, parsley, and corn syrup. Cover and bake in a 325° oven for 2 hours. Remove the cover for the last ½ hour of baking time. Serves 6–8.

Frijoles Negros

BLACK BEANS

2 *cups dried black beans*
1 *tablespoon salt*
3 *tablespoons olive oil*
1 *cup minced onions*
½ *teaspoon freshly ground black pepper*
1½ *cups milk*

Wash the beans and cover with water. Bring to a boil and let soak for 1 hour. Drain; add fresh water to cover. Bring to a boil and cook over low heat for 2 hours, or until tender. Add the salt after 1 hour. Drain, if any liquid remains.

Heat the oil in a skillet; brown the onions in it. Stir in the beans and pepper until coated. Add the milk and bring to a boil; cook until thick. Taste for seasoning. Serves 6–8.

Lentejas con Bananas

LENTILS AND BANANAS

1 *tablespoon olive oil*
2 *pounds pork, cubed*
¾ *cup chopped onions*
2 *cloves garlic, minced*
1½ *cups peeled, chopped tomatoes*
¼ *cup boiling water*
2½ *teaspoons salt*
¾ *teaspoon freshly ground black pepper*
1½ *cups lentils*
4 *cups water*
4 *firm bananas, cut into 1-inch pieces*
3 *tablespoons minced* cilantro (*coriander*) *or parsley*

[*over*]

Heat the oil in a casserole; brown the pork in it. Mix in the onions and garlic until browned. Add the tomatoes and boiling water, salt and pepper; cover and cook over low heat for 40 minutes. While the pork is cooking, prepare the lentils.

Wash lentils well and cook in the 4 cups water for 40 minutes. Add the undrained lentils to the pork. Mix well, cover, and cook over low heat for 30 minutes. Taste for seasoning. Add the bananas and *cilantro* or parsley; cook 5 minutes longer. Serves 6–8.

What one dish would you be most likely to encounter in a Paraguayan restaurant? It would most commonly be a *pasta*, one of the various types of spaghetti or other dough dishes of Italy. Find that difficult to follow? Actually, the reason is simple; much of Paraguay was settled by Italian immigrants, who naturally brought their native cuisine with them, to the delight of the local folk, who quickly adopted it as their own.

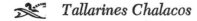 *Tallarines Chalacos*

BAKED SPAGHETTI WITH FISH SAUCE

1 cup olive or salad oil
1½ cups finely chopped onions
1 cup chopped red or green peppers
1 pound fillet of sole, snapper, or other white-meat fish
2 teaspoons salt
½ teaspoon dried ground chili peppers
1 pound spaghetti, cooked and drained
½ cup grated Parmesan cheese
2 tablespoons butter

Heat half the oil in a skillet; sauté the onions and green peppers for 10 minutes; add the remaining oil. Cut the fish in julienne strips and add to the vegetables with the salt and chili peppers. Cook over low heat for 10 minutes, stirring frequently. Taste for seasoning.

Put the spaghetti in a casserole, spread the fish mixture over it, sprinkle with the cheese, and dot with the butter. Bake in a 400° oven for 15 minutes. Serves 4.

Sopaipillas

CRISP FRITTERS

¼ *cup salad oil*
¼ *teaspoon salt*
¾ *cup lukewarm water*
1 egg, beaten
3 cups sifted flour
2 teaspoons baking powder
Fat for deep frying

Mix together the oil, salt, water, and egg. Sift the flour and baking powder twice and stir into the previous mixture; knead until smooth and elastic. Roll out as thin as possible and cut in narrow strips, circles, or any shape you like. Heat the fat to 375° and fry a few pieces at a time until browned. Drain and sprinkle with sugar. Serves 10–12.

EMPANADAS

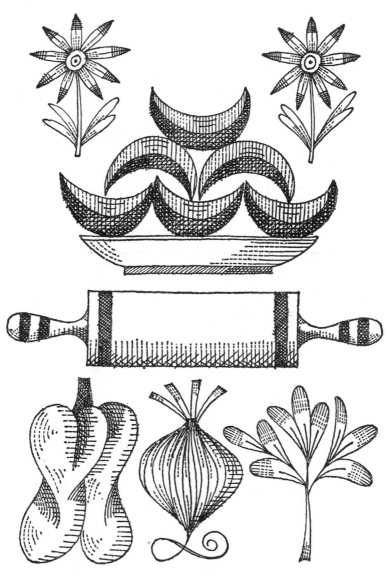

EMPANADAS

An *empanada*, basically, is pastry dough wrapped around any desired filling. In Brazil they're called *empadas*, but taste almost exactly the same. In much of South America these are the favorite between-meal snack, just as a frankfurter is in our own country. That's the starting point, but only the starting point, for an understanding or discussion of those delicious little pastries.

In Spanish-speaking countries, it is customary to shorten the names of one's friends, or to add little affectionate endings to their names, meaning "little" or "small." Thus, a girl named Rosa will usually be called Rosita, and so on. In that fashion, *empanadas* are also called *empanadillas*, or *empanaditas*, denoting littleness. But in point of fact, the terms are intermixed, and sometimes one *empanada* can be smaller than another *empanadilla*. What do the Brazilians call little *empadas*? *Empadinhas*.

⊰≋⊱ Empanadas de Carne

SMALL MEAT PIES

FILLING:

2 tablespoons butter
¾ cup chopped onions
¾ cup peeled, chopped tomatoes
½ cup chopped green peppers
¾ pound ground beef
1¼ teaspoons salt
¼ teaspoon dried ground chili peppers
2 hard-cooked eggs, chopped
3 tablespoons seedless raisins
½ cup chopped stuffed green olives

Melt the butter in a skillet; sauté the onions for 5 minutes. Add the tomatoes and green peppers; cook over low heat for 5 minutes. Stir in the beef, salt, and chili peppers until no pink remains in the meat. Remove from the heat and mix in the eggs, raisins, and olives; taste for seasoning and cool.

PASTRY:

2 cups sifted flour
1 teaspoon salt
¼ pound butter or lard
6 tablespoons ice water
Fat for deep frying

Sift the flour and salt into a bowl; cut in the butter, then stir in just enough of the water to form a ball of dough. Cover with a bowl and let stand for 15 minutes. Roll out on a lightly floured surface as thin as possible and cut in 5-inch circles. Place 1 tablespoon of the filling on each. Brush the edges with water and fold over the dough, pressing the edges together firmly.

Heat the fat to 360° and fry the pies until puffed, then increase heat to brown. Drain and serve hot or cold. Makes about 3 dozen.

Pastelitos de Puerco

PORK PASTRIES

2 *cups sifted flour*
¾ *cup butter*
⅔ *cup orange juice*
3 *tablespoons olive oil*
2 *tablespoons chopped onions*
2 *tablespoons chopped green peppers*
⅓ *clove garlic, minced*
¾ *pound ground pork*
1 *hard-cooked egg, mashed*
¼ *cup chopped green olives*
¼ *cup seedless raisins*
1½ *teaspoons salt*
¼ *teaspoon freshly ground black pepper*

Sift the flour into a bowl; cut in the butter with a pastry blender or 2 knives. Stir in the orange juice until a ball of dough is formed. Chill while preparing the pork.

Heat the oil in a skillet; sauté the onions, green peppers, garlic, and pork until no pink remains in the pork. Mix in the egg, olives, raisins, salt, and pepper. Cook for 5 minutes; taste for seasoning and cool.

Roll out the dough as thin as possible; cut into 2-inch circles with a cooky cutter. Place a tablespoon of the pork mixture on half the circles and cover with the remaining circles. Seal the edges with a little water. Arrange on a baking sheet. Brush tops with cream or beaten egg yolks. Bake in a preheated 425° oven for 15 minutes, or until browned. Serve hot. Makes about 18.

Empadinhas de Camarões

SHRIMP PASTRIES

1½ cups sifted flour
2 teaspoons salt
¾ cup shortening
1 egg, beaten
¼ cup ice water
3 tablespoons olive oil
½ cup chopped onions
1½ cups chopped tomatoes
¾ pound cooked shrimp, diced
½ teaspoon freshly ground black pepper
2 hard-cooked egg yolks, chopped
¼ cup chopped black olives
2 tablespoons minced parsley

Sift the flour and ¾ teaspoon salt into a bowl; cut in the shortening with a pastry blender or 2 knives. Stir in the egg and water until a ball of dough is formed. Chill for 2 hours.

Heat the oil in a skillet; sauté the onions for 10 minutes. Add the tomatoes; cook over low heat for 10 minutes. Mix in the shrimp, pepper, and remaining salt; cook over low heat for 5 minutes. Remove from heat and blend in the egg yolks, olives, and parsley. Taste for seasoning and cool for 15 minutes.

Roll out the dough on a lightly floured surface ⅛ inch thick. Cut into 5-inch circles. Place a tablespoon of the shrimp mixture on each, and fold over the dough, sealing the edges with a little water. Arrange on a buttered baking sheet. Bake in a preheated 400° oven for 15 minutes, or until browned. Makes about 2 dozen.

Empanadas de Queso

CHEESE PASTRIES

2½ cups sifted flour
½ teaspoon salt
1 teaspoon sugar
1 teaspoon baking powder
¾ cup shortening
4 egg yolks
½ cup milk
2 egg whites
2 cups grated Cheddar cheese
1 teaspoon Spanish paprika

Sift the flour, salt, sugar, and baking powder into a bowl; cut in the shortening. Beat the egg yolks and milk together; stir into the flour mixture until a ball of dough is formed. Chill for 1 hour. Preheat oven to 375°.

Beat the egg whites until frothy; stir in the cheese and paprika. Roll out the dough as thin as possible on a lightly floured surface. Cut into 3-inch circles. Place a teaspoon of the cheese mixture on half the circles and cover with the remaining circles; press the edges together firmly. Place on a baking sheet. Bake for 15 minutes, or until browned. Serve hot. Makes about 3 dozen.

 Cacerola de Tortillas

TORTILLA CASSEROLE

18 tortillas
½ pound cream cheese
3 cups cooked, shredded chicken or turkey
1 cup grated Parmesan cheese
1½ cups heavy cream

Spread the *tortillas* with cream cheese, then with the chicken or turkey. Fold over. In a buttered casserole, arrange layers of the

[*over*]

tortillas sprinkled with the Parmesan cheese. Pour the cream over all. Cover and bake in a preheated 350° oven for 30 minutes. Remove cover and bake 10 minutes longer. Serves 8–10.

༺ᐳᐃ᠊ *Enchiladas Verdes*

GREEN ENCHILADAS

1 cup olive oil
1 pound ground pork
¼ teaspoon orégano
2 cloves garlic, minced
3 green peppers, sliced
1 cup water
2 cups diced green tomatoes
2 cups diced onions
3 tablespoons minced cilantro *(coriander) or parsley*
2½ teaspoons salt
¼ teaspoon dried ground chili peppers
½ cup heavy cream
18 tortillas
2 cups grated American cheese
1 cup chopped onions

Heat ¼ cup oil in a skillet; sauté the pork, orégano, and garlic until browned. Cover and cook over low heat until no pink remains in the pork. Add a little water if necessary to keep from burning.

Cook the peppers in the water until tender. Drain, reserving the water. Cook the tomatoes over low heat for 5 minutes. Grind together to a paste the green peppers, tomatoes, diced onions and *cilantro* or parsley. Heat the remaining oil in a skillet; sauté the paste for 15 minutes, stirring frequently. Add the reserved water, pork, salt, and chili peppers. Sauté 5 minutes longer. Mix in the cream.

Spread the *tortillas* with the grated cheese and sprinkle with chopped onions. Fold over and place 2 or 3 in a plate. Spoon the sauce over them. Serves 6–9.

VEGETABLES

VEGETABLES

The potato, which we habitually regard as Irish, was originally grown in South America and brought back to Europe by the sixteenth- and seventeenth-century explorers. It became a great boon to the Old World, where an easily produced, almost sure crop was greatly in demand. Incidentally, the South American manner of treating potatoes is extraordinarily interesting. *Papas à la Huancaina*, the classic Peruvian potato dish, is particularly noteworthy.

Almost all of South America was originally settled by either Portuguese or Spanish nationals, to whom a vegetable without onions and tomatoes is hardly worth mentioning. To these national styles the venturesome touches of native and African cooks were added. The result: unusual and delicious vegetable recipes.

Vegetables for Panagra's Lima Commissary are specially grown at a mountain farm high up in the Andes, at an altitude of 4500 feet, because of the crystal-clear pure water found there.

Papas con Tomates
POTATOES WITH TOMATOES

8 potatoes (3 pounds)
4 tablespoons butter
1 cup minced onions
¼ teaspoon dried ground chili peppers
2 teaspoons salt
1½ cups peeled chopped tomatoes
1 cup canned corn kernels
½ cup hot milk

Peel the potatoes and cut in half; cook until tender but firm. Drain well. Melt the butter in a skillet; sauté the onions and chili peppers for 5 minutes. Add the salt and tomatoes. Cook over low heat for 10 minutes. Add the corn. Cook for 5 minutes. Mash 2 of the potato halves with the milk and mix into the tomato mixture, then add the remaining potatoes, mixing until well coated. Serves 8.

Papas à la Huancaina
POTATOES IN CHEESE SAUCE, PERUVIAN MANNER

½ pound cream cheese
4 hard-cooked egg yolks
1 teaspoon salt
¼ teaspoon dried ground chili peppers
¼ cup olive oil
1 cup light cream
½ cup finely chopped onions
6 potatoes, cooked, cooled, and sliced
12 black olives

Cream the cheese with a wooden spoon, gradually working in the egg yolks. Mix in the salt and chili peppers. Beat in the oil, by the teaspoon, then the cream, and finally the onions. Pour over the potatoes and garnish with the olives. Serves 6–8.

 *Capirotada de Papas*

POTATO CASSEROLE

2 pounds potatoes, peeled and sliced thin
1½ cups sliced onions
4 tablespoons butter
2 teaspoons salt
½ teaspoon freshly ground black pepper
4 slices buttered toast
1½ cups tomato juice
½ cup grated Parmesan cheese
2 tablespoons dry bread crumbs

Sauté the potatoes and onions in the butter until browned. Sprinkle with the salt and pepper. Cut the toast in narrow strips and arrange on the bottom of a buttered casserole. Spread some sautéed vegetables over them, and moisten with some tomato juice. Repeat layers until ingredients are all used up. Sprinkle with the cheese and bread crumbs. Bake in 350° oven for 25 minutes, or until browned. Serves 4–6.

Emparedado

FRIED-POTATO CROQUETTES

1½ cups mashed potatoes or 1 envelope instant mashed
  potatoes
1 cup sifted flour
1 cup sour cream
2 eggs, beaten
½ teaspoon baking soda
½ teaspoon white pepper
4 tablespoons butter
½ cup chopped stuffed green olives
¼ cup minced parsley

[over]

If instant mashed potatoes are used, prepare the potatoes as package directs, using only ¾ of the milk specified; cool. Stir in the flour, sour cream, eggs, baking soda, and pepper.

Melt the butter in a skillet; drop the potato mixture into it by the heaping tablespoon. Fry until browned on both sides. Sprinkle with the olives and parsley. Makes about a dozen.

The Indians of Bolivia are particularly fond of *chuño,* a frozen potato. Because of the high altitudes, the locally grown potatoes are quite small to begin with, but the Indians successively freeze and thaw the potatoes several times. The net result is a darkish, dried-up potato about the general size and shape of a golf ball, consisting almost entirely of starch, since most of the natural water of the potato has been removed by freezing and thawing. The resulting flavor is quite appealing, vaguely reminiscent of a mild cheese in taste and texture. Regular potatoes are prepared in interesting ways too, as in the following recipe.

Patatas Rellenos con Queso

POTATO-CHEESE CROQUETTES

3 cups mashed potatoes or 2 envelopes instant mashed potatoes
2 egg yolks
1½ teaspoons chili powder
¼ pound cream cheese
1 egg, beaten
1 cup dry bread crumbs
Fat for deep frying

If instant mashed potatoes are used, prepare the potatoes as package directs, using only ¾ the amount of liquid. Beat in the egg yolks and chili powder. Taste for seasoning. Shape into 1½-inch balls. Make a depression in each and place a teaspoon of cream cheese in it. Cover with the potatoes; roll in the egg and then in the bread crumbs.

Heat the fat to 370°. Fry a few balls at a time until browned. Drain well. Makes about a dozen.

 *Patatas Coloradas*

POTATOES IN RED SAUCE

2 tablespoons olive oil
¾ cup chopped onions
1½ cups canned tomatoes
1½ teaspoons salt
¼ teaspoon dried ground chili peppers
4 potatoes, cooked, drained, and quartered
2 tablespoons minced parsley

Heat the oil in a saucepan; sauté the onions for 10 minutes. Add the tomatoes, salt, and chili peppers. Cook over low heat for 45 minutes. Purée in an electric blender or force through a sieve. Return to the saucepan, add potatoes, bring to a boil, sprinkle with parsley, and serve. Serves 4–6.

Potatoes are moderately popular throughout South America, but most people prefer to eat the locally grown plátano, *the plantain, which comes in many different sizes and species. Plantains have a pleasantly starchy taste, roughly resembling a cross of a white potato, a sweet potato, and a banana; it is cooked while in varying stages of maturity —completely green, half developed, or completely ripe— each producing a somewhat different flavor. Other popular root plants include the* yuca, *the cassava plant;* name, *a sort of yam;* boniato, *a mealy type of sweet potato;* fruta de pan, *the famous breadfruit of the tropics. In parts of South America corn is extraordinarily popular, particularly with the Indian population, but in other parts of the continent its importance is not nearly so great. However, rice is a great staple and national favorite in every country.*

Frituras de Yautia

SWEET-POTATO FRITTERS

4 sweet potatoes
1 tablespoon cornstarch
1 teaspoon baking powder
1 teaspoon salt
¼ teaspoon nutmeg
2 eggs, beaten
¼ cup oil or shortening

Bake the potatoes until tender, then mash the pulp. Measure 3 cups and mix with the cornstarch, baking powder, salt, nutmeg, and eggs.

Heat the oil in a skillet and drop the mixture into it by the heaping tablespoon. Fry until browned on both sides. Makes about 30.

Tomates Asados

BAKED TOMATOES

6 tomatoes
½ cup corn meal
2 tablespoons flour
1 teaspoon salt
¼ teaspoon freshly ground black pepper
3 tablespoons grated onions
3 tablespoons olive oil

Buy firm, even-size tomatoes. Cut in half crosswise. Mix together the corn meal, flour, salt, pepper, and onions. Brush the tomatoes with the oil, and then spread the corn-meal mixture on the cut side. Arrange in a greased baking dish; bake in a 425° oven for 20 minutes, or until browned and tender. Serves 6–12.

Tomates Rellenos

STUFFED TOMATOES

8 *tomatoes*
2 *tablespoons butter*
½ *cup chopped onions*
1¼ *cups canned corn kernels*
2 *eggs, beaten*
1¼ *teaspoons salt*
⅛ *teaspoon Tabasco*
½ *cup grated Cheddar cheese*
2 *tablespoons chopped pimientos*

Buy large, firm tomatoes. Cut a ½-inch piece from the stem end of the tomatoes and reserve. Carefully scoop out the pulp. Melt the butter in a skillet; sauté the onions for 5 minutes. Add the tomato pulp and cook over low heat for 5 minutes. Cool for 5 minutes. Mix in the corn, eggs, salt, Tabasco, cheese, and pimientos. Stuff the tomatoes. Cover with the reserved pieces. Arrange in a buttered baking dish. Bake in a 375° oven for 35 minutes, or until tender. Serves 8.

Capirotada de Calabacitas

SQUASH CASSEROLE

3 *pounds yellow squash*
3 *tablespoons butter*
1 *cup thinly sliced onions*
1 *teaspoon salt*
¼ *teaspoon nutmeg*
4 *slices buttered toast*
1½ *cups milk*
½ *cup grated American cheese*
3 *tablespoons dry bread crumbs*

[over]

Cut the unpeeled squash in ¼-inch slices. Cook in boiling water for 10 minutes. Drain well and dry.

Melt the butter in a skillet; sauté the onions, salt, and nutmeg for 10 minutes. Cut the toast in narrow strips and cover the bottom of a buttered casserole with them. Arrange some squash slices over them; spread some onions on top and moisten with some milk. Repeat layers until ingredients are used up. Sprinkle with the cheese and bread crumbs. Bake in a 350° oven for 30 minutes, or until browned. Serves 4–6.

⚞ *Calabaza con Maíz*

SQUASH AND CORN

3 pounds yellow squash
2 teaspoons salt
4 tablespoons butter
½ cup chopped onions
2 teaspoons Spanish paprika
1½ cups fresh or canned corn kernels
2 eggs, beaten
¼ cup grated Parmesan cheese

Peel and cube the squash. Combine with the salt in a saucepan; cover and cook over low heat for 30 minutes, or until soft. Watch carefully to prevent burning and add a little water if necessary.

Melt the butter in a skillet; sauté the onions for 5 minutes. Stir in the paprika and corn; cook over low heat for 5 minutes. Add to the squash; cook over low heat for 5 minutes. Beat in the eggs and cheese. Serves 4–6.

 *Calabaza y Queso*

BAKED SQUASH AND CHEESE

2 pounds yellow squash
2 teaspoons salt
¼ pound cream cheese
2 tablespoons minced parsley
½ cup melted butter

Select small, uniform-size squash. Pare lightly and cut in half lengthwise. Arrange in a deep skillet and almost cover with water. Add the salt, cover the skillet, and bring to a boil; cook over medium heat for 10 minutes. Drain well.

Have the cream cheese at room temperature and blend in the parsley. Spread on the cut halves of the squash and put the halves together. Arrange in a buttered baking dish; pour the butter over them. Bake in a 375° oven for 20 minutes, or until browned. Cut in half crosswise. Serves 6–8.

Chauchas

GREEN BEANS AND POTATOES

1 cup water
1½ pounds green beans, quartered, or 2 packages frozen
1 teaspoon salt
2 tablespoons olive oil
3 tablespoons lemon juice
1 tablespoon minced onions
1 envelope instant mashed potatoes
Dash cayenne pepper
1 egg yolk, beaten
2 pimientos, cut julienne

[over]

Bring the water to a boil; add the beans and salt. Cook fresh beans for 15 minutes, or until tender but firm, or frozen beans as package directs. Drain well; toss with the oil, lemon juice, and onions. Heap in a deep serving dish. While the beans are cooking, prepare the potatoes as package directs. Beat in the cayenne pepper and egg yolk. Cover the beans with the potato mixture and arrange pimientos on top. Serves 6–8.

Pastel de Espinaca

BAKED SPINACH ROLL

2⅛ cups sifted flour
¼ teaspoon salt
2 tablespoons sugar
½ pound butter
2 egg yolks, beaten
2 tablespoons water
2 packages frozen chopped spinach
¾ cup heavy cream
¼ teaspoon white pepper
2 hard-cooked eggs, sliced
¼ cup seedless raisins

Sift 2 cups flour, the salt and sugar into a bowl. Cut in the butter with a pastry blender or 2 knives. Stir in the egg yolks and water until a ball of dough is formed. Chill for 1 hour.

Cook the spinach as the package directs; drain well. Mix in the remaining flour, then the cream and pepper. Cook over low heat for 5 minutes, stirring frequently. Taste for seasoning. Cool while dough is chilling.

Roll out the dough as thin as possible. Spread the spinach over it and arrange the sliced eggs and raisins on the spinach. Roll up like a jelly roll; place on a baking sheet. Bake in a preheated 375° oven for 30 minutes, or until delicately browned. Slice and serve hot. Serves 8–10.

Berenjenais con Tomates

BAKED EGGPLANT WITH TOMATOES

1 eggplant
½ cup flour
2½ teaspoons salt
¾ teaspoon freshly ground black pepper
3 tablespoons olive oil
3 tablespoons bread crumbs
4 tomatoes, peeled and sliced thin
1 teaspoon sugar
3 tablespoons grated Parmesan cheese
2 tablespoons melted butter

Buy a large eggplant; peel and slice ½ inch thick. Mix together the flour, 1½ teaspoons salt, and ¼ teaspoon pepper. Dip the slices in the mixture and sauté in the oil until browned on both sides. Arrange in a baking dish; sprinkle with the bread crumbs, and cover with the tomato slices. Sprinkle with the sugar, the remaining salt and pepper, the cheese and butter. Bake in a 350° oven for 25 minutes. Serves 4–6.

 Guiso de Ejotes

GREEN BEANS IN TOMATO SAUCE

2 tablespoons olive oil
¾ cup chopped onions
1 clove garlic, minced
2 cups canned tomatoes
2 teaspoons salt
¼ teaspoon dried ground chili peppers
2 pounds green beans, or 2 packages frozen
3 tablespoons minced pimientos
2 tablespoons minced parsley   [*over*]

Heat the oil in a saucepan; sauté the onions for 5 minutes. Add the garlic, tomatoes, salt, and chili peppers. Cook over low heat for 30 minutes. Add the beans—cook fresh beans for 45 minutes, frozen for 25. Mix in the pimientos and parsley; cook 5 minutes longer. Taste for seasoning. Serves 6–8.

≫⋙ *Espinaca al Horno*

BAKED SPINACH

3 *pounds spinach or 3 packages frozen, thawed*
1½ *cups chopped onions*
1 *cup chopped green peppers*
2 *teaspoons salt*
¼ *teaspoon dried ground chili peppers*
6 *tablespoons butter*
¼ *cup seedless raisins, chopped*
2 *teaspoons sugar*
⅓ *cup tomato juice*
¼ *cup grated Parmesan cheese*

If fresh spinach is used, discard the stems and wash thoroughly. Combine fresh or frozen spinach, onions, green peppers, salt, and chili peppers in a saucepan. Cover and cook over low heat for 5 minutes. Drain and chop fine. Add 3 tablespoons butter, the raisins, sugar, and tomato juice. Turn into a buttered baking dish, sprinkle with the cheese, and dot with the remaining butter. Bake in a 400° oven for 10 minutes, or until delicately browned. Serves 4–6.

 *Guisantes con Cebollas*

PEAS AND ONIONS

4 tablespoons butter
1 cup finely chopped onions
½ cup finely chopped green peppers
1 tablespoon minced parsley
¼ teaspoon nutmeg
1 teaspoon lemon juice
4 pounds green peas, shelled, or 2 packages frozen
1 bay leaf
1½ teaspoons salt
½ cup boiling water

Melt the butter in a skillet; sauté the onions for 5 minutes. Add the green peppers and parsley. Sauté over very low heat until soft but not browned. Stir in the nutmeg and lemon juice.

Cook the peas with the bay leaf and salt in the boiling water until tender but firm. Drain well and add to the sautéed vegetables. Toss until well coated. Serves 4–6.

Chilis Fritos

FRIED GREEN PEPPERS

8 green peppers
¾ cup sifted flour
¼ teaspoon salt
1 teaspoon baking powder
1 egg
⅓ cup milk
Fat for deep frying

[over]

Cut the peppers in half lengthwise; scoop out the seeds and fibers. Sift the flour, salt, and baking powder into a bowl. Beat the egg and milk; add to the flour mixture, stirring until smooth. Dip the peppers into the batter. Heat the fat to 365° and fry the peppers in it until tender and browned. Serves 8–10.

Cebollas en Salsa de Tomate

BAKED ONIONS IN TOMATO SAUCE

3 tablespoons olive oil
1 cup chopped green peppers
1½ pounds small white onions
3 cups canned tomato sauce
1½ teaspoons salt
½ teaspoon freshly ground black pepper
¼ teaspoon ground coriander

Heat the oil in a casserole; sauté the green peppers and onions for 10 minutes, shaking the casserole frequently. Add the tomato sauce, salt, pepper, and coriander. Cover and bake in a 350° oven for 50 minutes. Serves 6–8.

The pachamanca *is the gayest and liveliest of all Peruvian food customs. Actually, it is a combination barbecue, picnic, and fiesta rolled into one.*
An oven made of stones is constructed on the spot of the pachamanca, *each stone being washed carefully and then*

fitted into place to form a cone. A strong fire is made to heat up the stones until they are red-hot.

The oven is filled with seasoned meats and poultry, vegetables wrapped in banana leaves, some fresh cheeses; and the "oven" is then covered with large, ripe banana leaves. Additional hot stones are then placed on top, and the entire affair is covered with earth, with only a small opening for the steam to escape. While the food is cooking, everyone dances the local dances of the region, usually the strong huaynitos or the dashing marinera. With the delicious food of the pachamanca, everyone drinks chicha de jora, a type of Indian beer.

 Berenjenas Rellenas

STUFFED EGGPLANT

3 small eggplants
6 tablespoons olive oil
1½ cups chopped onions
1 cup chopped green peppers
2 teaspoons salt
¼ teaspoon dried ground chili peppers
1¼ cups dry bread crumbs
½ cup sliced stuffed green olives
1 cup chicken broth
3 tablespoons butter

Cut the eggplants in half lengthwise. Scoop out the pulp and dice; reserve the shells. Heat the oil in a skillet; sauté the eggplant pulp, onions, and green peppers for 10 minutes. Sprinkle with the salt and chili peppers. Cook for 2 minutes. Mix in 1 cup bread crumbs, the olives and the broth. Taste for seasoning. Stuff the shells, sprinkle with the remaining crumbs, and dot with the butter. Place in a baking pan containing 1 inch of water. Bake in a 350° oven for 35 minutes. Serves 6.

≋ *Olla Gitana*

GYPSY VEGETABLE STEW

4 tablespoons olive oil
1 cup chopped onions
1 cup diced tomatoes
1 tablespoon flour
1½ pounds green beans, quartered
1 parsnip, sliced
4 cups water
2 cups diced eggplant
2 cups diced zucchini
2 teaspoons salt
¼ teaspoon dried ground chili peppers

Heat the oil in a saucepan; sauté the onions for 10 minutes. Add the tomatoes and flour; cook over medium heat for 2 minutes, stirring steadily. Add the beans, parsnip, water, eggplant, zucchini, salt, and chili peppers. Bring to a boil and cook over low heat for 1¼ hours. Serves 6–8.

SALADS AND SAUCES

SALADS AND SAUCES 🐟

In most of South America, the traditional green salad is seldom encountered, except in international-style hotels and restaurants. A family dinner, more than likely, will not ordinarily include a salad course. As a generalization, it may be said that most Latins have taken to serving salads only in recent years.

Of course there were always exceptions, particularly in Brazil, where hearts-of-palm salad have always been popular. Also, wherever the luscious avocados grow, there have always been gourmets to make avocado salads. Thus, we find a whole series of salads based upon whole, sliced, or chopped avocados, usually served with a sharp, tangy dressing. The Mexicans are notably fond of *Guacamole*, the famous spicy avocado mixture, which is made in a hundred (or more!) different ways. Originally, this dish was called *aguacamole*, based upon the Spanish word for avocado, *aguacate*.

⟩⟨ Ensalada de Aguacate

AVOCADO SALAD

½ cup olive or salad oil
¼ cup wine vinegar
1 teaspoon salt
½ teaspoon freshly ground black pepper
½ teaspoon dry mustard
1 clove garlic, minced
3 avocados
½ cup chopped pimientos
Lettuce

Beat together the oil, vinegar, salt, pepper, mustard, and garlic. Cut the avocados in half lengthwise and remove the pits. Prick the flesh of the fruit in several places. Pour the dressing into the avocado halves and sprinkle with the pimientos. Serve on lettuce. Serves 6.

⟩⟨ Ensalada de Aguacate de Vera Cruz

VERA CRUZ AVOCADO SALAD

¾ cup olive oil
¼ cup wine vinegar
1½ teaspoons salt
½ teaspoon freshly ground black pepper
2 teaspoons Spanish paprika
3 tomatoes, diced
½ cup chopped scallions (green onions)
2 tablespoons minced parsley
⅛ teaspoon dried ground chili peppers
3 avocados

Mix together the oil, vinegar, salt, pepper, and paprika. Toss together tomatoes, scallions, parsley, and chili peppers. Cut the avocados in half lengthwise. Cut the pulp away from the skin gently, but leave it in the skin. Fill with tomato mixture and pour dressing over all. Serves 6.

 Ensalada de Guacamole

GUACAMOLE SALAD

2 avocados
1 cup peeled, diced tomatoes
2 hard-cooked eggs, diced
½ cup sliced, stuffed olives
¼ cup minced onions
⅓ cup olive oil
2 tablespoons cider vinegar
1¼ teaspoons salt
¼ teaspoon dried ground chili peppers
Lettuce
4 slices crisp bacon, crumbled

Peel and dice the avocados; mix with the tomatoes, eggs, olives, onions, oil, vinegar, salt, and chili peppers. Heap on lettuce leaves and sprinkle the bacon on top. Serves 4–6.

 Ensalada de Aguacate y Papas

AVOCADO-POTATO SALAD

4 slices bacon
3 cups cooked diced potatoes
½ cup chopped onions
2 hard-cooked eggs, chopped
1 teaspoon salt
½ teaspoon freshly ground black pepper
½ cup mayonnaise
2 tablespoons lemon juice
2 avocados, peeled and cubed

[over]

Fry the bacon crisp; drain and crumble. Toss together the potatoes, onions, eggs, salt, pepper, and bacon. Fold in the mayonnaise mixed with the lemon juice, then toss in the avocado. Serves 6–10.

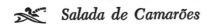 *Ensalada Amoldada de Aguacate*

MOLDED AVOCADO SALAD

1 envelope (tablespoon) gelatin
¼ cup boiling water
2 avocados
¾ teaspoon salt
2 tablespoons grated onion
2 tablespoons minced pimiento
4 drops Tabasco
1 tablespoon lime or lemon juice

Dissolve the gelatin in the boiling water. Cool for 15 minutes. Cut the avocados in half lengthwise and scoop out the pulp; reserve the shells. Mash the pulp smooth; blend in the gelatin, salt, onion, pimiento, Tabasco, and lime juice. Refill the shells and chill until firm. Serve with mayonnaise mixed with whipped cream, if desired. Serves 4.

Salada de Camarões

SHRIMP SALAD

1 pound shrimp, cooked, cleaned, and chopped
2 avocados, peeled and diced
2 tablespoons lemon juice
½ cup chopped green olives
¾ cup mayonnaise
Lettuce
2 hard-cooked eggs, chopped

Toss together the shrimp, avocados, lemon juice, olives, and ½ cup mayonnaise. Taste for seasoning, adding salt and pepper if necessary. Heap on lettuce leaves and place a spoon of mayonnaise on top. Sprinkle with the eggs. Serves 4–6.

Paltas Rellenas

STUFFED AVOCADOS

2 potatoes (1 pound) or 1 envelope instant mashed potatoes
2 tablespoons grated onions
⅛ teaspoon dried ground chili peppers
¼ cup olive oil
2 drops yellow food coloring
3 avocado pears
1 tablespoon lemon juice
Lettuce
12 shrimp, cooked and cleaned
12 black olives
3 sweet corn, cooked

Cook the potatoes in salted water, drain, and mash very smooth. Or prepare instant mashed potatoes as package directs. Mix in the onions, chili peppers, olive oil, and food coloring. (In Peru, yellow potatoes are used.)

Cut the avocados in half, remove the pits, and peel. Sprinkle with the lemon juice. Place on lettuce leaves and fill with the potato mixture. Arrange the shrimp and olives on top. Cut the corn in 2-inch pieces and place around the avocados. Serves 6.

Ensalada de Langosta

LOBSTER SALAD

1 pound cooked lobster meat
½ cup olive or salad oil
3 tablespoons lime or lemon juice
½ teaspoon salt
4 drops Tabasco
4 tablespoons minced onion
¾ cup diced celery
½ cup mayonnaise
¼ cup whipped cream
Water cress
1 cup sliced stuffed olives

Cube the lobster; marinate for 1 hour in a mixture of the oil, lime or lemon juice, salt, and Tabasco. Drain well; toss with the onion and celery, then with the mayonnaise and whipped cream. Form into mounds on the water cress and decorate with the olives. Serves 4–6.

 Ensalada de Frijoles

BEAN SALAD

3 pimientos, minced
¾ cup chopped green peppers
½ cup chopped scallions (green onions)
½ cup diced cucumbers
2 teaspoons minced garlic
2 cups cooked or canned red beans
¾ cup French dressing
Lettuce or water cress

Toss all the ingredients together and let marinate for 1 hour before serving on lettuce or water cress. Serves 6–8.

Pebre

TOMATO-ONION SALAD

3 cups cubed tomatoes
2 cups finely chopped sweet onions
1 canned Jalapeño pepper, minced, or ¼ teaspoon dried ground chili peppers
⅔ cup olive oil
3 tablespoons wine vinegar
1½ teaspoons salt
Lettuce cups

Toss together the tomatoes, onions, and chili peppers. Mix together the oil, vinegar, and salt; pour over the vegetables. Chill for 1 hour before serving in lettuce cups. Serves 4–6.

 Ensalada para Arroz con Pollo

SALAD TO SERVE WITH RICE AND CHICKEN

3 cups shredded lettuce
2 tomatoes, sliced
12 anchovies
¼ cup sliced green olives
¼ cup sliced black olives
6 thin slices onion
¾ cup French dressing

On each plate, heap ½ cup of lettuce. Arrange tomatoes, anchovies, olives, and onion slices over it. Pour the dressing over all. Serves 6.

Ensalada de Garbanzas

CHICK-PEA SALAD

1 cup dried chick-peas
3 teaspoons salt
½ cup olive oil
¼ cup lemon juice
¼ teaspoon freshly ground black pepper
½ teaspoon ground coriander
½ pound cream cheese, diced
¾ cup thinly sliced onions
Lettuce
3 hard-cooked eggs, quartered

Wash the chick-peas, cover with water, and bring to a boil; let soak for 1 hour. Drain, add fresh water to cover, bring to a boil, and cook over low heat for 2 hours, or until tender. Add 2 teaspoons salt after 1 hour. Drain well and cool (2 cups canned chick-peas may be substituted, in which case just drain them).

Beat together the oil, lemon juice, pepper, coriander, and remaining salt. In a bowl, toss together the chick-peas, cream cheese, and onions. Pour the dressing over the mixture and mix lightly. Arrange on lettuce and garnish with the quartered eggs. Serves 4–6.

Fish is extremely plentiful along much of South America's generous coastline. Often, there is so much fish, that the leftovers are used in making a fish salad.

 Ensalada de Pescado

FISH SALAD

1½ *pounds white-meat fish*
1 *onion*
3 *cups water*
3 *teaspoons salt*
½ *teaspoon white pepper*
½ *cup thinly sliced scallions (green onions)*
1 *cup chopped celery*
¾ *cup diced tomatoes*
¼ *cup minced green peppers*
¼ *cup chopped stuffed olives*
¾ *cup mayonnaise*
Water cress or lettuce

Combine the fish, onion, water, 2 teaspoons salt, and ¼ teaspoon pepper in a saucepan. Bring to a boil and cook over low heat for 25 minutes. Drain well, flake, and cool.

Toss together the scallions, celery, tomatoes, green peppers, olives, fish, and remaining salt and pepper. Fold in the mayonnaise. Serve on water cress or lettuce. Serves 6–8.

Ensalada de Legumbres

VEGETABLE-AND-SAUSAGE SALAD

½ *pound Spanish or Italian sausages, sliced*
2 *packages frozen mixed vegetables*
1 *head romaine lettuce*
2 *tomatoes, peeled and sliced*
¼ *cup chopped scallions (green onions)*
½ *cup olive oil*
⅓ *cup wine vinegar*
1½ *teaspoons salt*
½ *teaspoon freshly ground black pepper*
1 *clove garlic, minced*
3 *tablespoons minced parsley*

Fry the sausages until browned. Drain and cool. Cook the vegetables 1 minute less than the package directs. Drain and cool. Break the lettuce into small pieces and toss with the mixed vegetables, tomatoes, scallions, and sausages.

Beat together the oil, vinegar, salt, pepper, garlic, and parsley. Pour over the vegetables and mix lightly. Chill for 1 hour. Serves 6–8.

 Salsa de Mangos

MANGO SAUCE

3 *firm mangoes*
2 *tablespoons sugar*

Prepare mango sauce when the fruit is reasonable. It's a delightful change from applesauce.

Peel and dice the mangoes. Add the sugar. Cook over low heat until soft. Watch carefully to prevent burning. Purée in an electric blender or force through a sieve. Taste for sweetening. Serve warm or cold. Makes about 2 cups.

Condimento de Ají

PEPPER RELISH

12 green peppers
12 red peppers
12 onions
2 cups white vinegar
1 cup sugar
2 tablespoons salt
¾ teaspoon dried ground chili peppers
1 teaspoon celery seed
1 teaspoon mustard seed

Chop together or grind, using the medium blade of a food chopper, the peppers and onions. Cover with boiling water and let stand for 5 minutes. Drain thoroughly, then add the vinegar, sugar, salt, chili peppers, celery, and mustard seed. Bring to a boil and cook over low heat for 3 minutes. Pack into sterile jars and let stand for 3 days before serving. Makes about 3 pints.

 Salsa de Aguacate para Pescado

AVOCADO SAUCE FOR FISH

2 avocados
3 tablespoons olive oil
3 tablespoons lemon juice
1 tablespoon cider vinegar
1 teaspoon salt
¼ teaspoon white pepper
2 teaspoons grated onion

Scoop out the pulp of the avocados and purée in an electric blender or force through a sieve. Beat in the oil, lemon juice, vinegar, salt, pepper, and onion juice until the mixture has the consistency of mayonnaise. Serve with boiled or fried fish. Makes about 2 cups.

DESSERTS

AND

BEVERAGES

DESSERTS AND BEVERAGES 🐟

South American desserts differ substantially from ours. Cakes and pies, the favorite American desserts, are comparatively rare, but puddings, pastries, fried sweet creams, custards, and fruit preparations are extremely popular. It is not that Latins do not enjoy desserts, but rather that they have somewhat different tastes from ours.

About five each afternoon—the classic tea hour—men and women head for the *confiterías*, the attractive pastry houses so popular throughout the continent. There they enjoy numerous (to say the least!) pastries and several cups of tea, coffee, or chocolate. The teatime snack is an absolute necessity in South American countries, where the earliest dinner hour is 8 P.M., and may easily be delayed until eleven or even midnight.

Quesadillas

LITTLE CHEESECAKES

1 *cup sugar*
2 *cups sifted rice flour or cornstarch*
½ *pound butter*
2 *eggs*
6 *egg whites*
8 *egg yolks*

Preheat oven to 350°.
Sift the sugar and flour or cornstarch together; work in the butter, then beat in the 2 eggs until very light. Beat the egg whites until stiff but not dry. Beat the egg yolks until thick, and fold into the egg whites. Mix into the dough lightly. Divide among paper cupcake cups. Bake for 20 minutes, or until browned and set. Cool. Makes about 20.

Venezuela was so named by the Spanish explorers who discovered this country, because they found the Indian natives living in straw huts perched on stilts above the waters of the river. What could be more natural than to call it "Little Venice," or Venezuela?

Torta Criolla de Queso

VENEZUELAN CHEESE CAKE

8 *egg yolks*
1 *cup sugar*
1 *pound cream cheese*
1 *teaspoon baking powder*
8 *egg whites, stiffly beaten*

Preheat oven to 375°.

Beat the egg yolks and sugar until thick and light. Have the cheese at room temperature and beat in. Stir in the baking powder; then fold in the egg whites thoroughly. Turn into a buttered, 8-inch spring-form pan. Bake for 45 minutes, or until a cake tester comes out clean. Cool. Serves 8–12.

Bananas are often served instead of potatoes in many parts of South America, sometimes baked, occasionally fried, or in several other fashions. After a stay of several months, foreigners are said to have become *abananada*—that is, bananaized, or accustomed to living in the particular country.

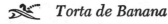 *Torta de Banana*

BANANA TART

5 *bananas*
⅛ *teaspoon salt*
½ *cup sugar*
2 *tablespoons butter*
2 *tablespoons lime or lemon juice*
½ *teaspoon nutmeg*
1 *cup whipped cream*
1 *8-inch baked pastry shell*

Mash the bananas very smooth, or purée in an electric blender. Combine with the salt, sugar, and butter in a saucepan; bring to a boil. Cool and fold in the lime or lemon juice, nutmeg, and whipped cream. Turn into the pie shell. Chill. Serves 6–8.

Pastel de Platano

BANANA PIE

6 *bananas*
½ *cup sugar*
1 *tablespoon melted butter*
½ *cup ground almonds*
1 *cup chopped seedless raisins*
1 *teaspoon cinnamon*
¼ *teaspoon nutmeg*
½ *teaspoon powdered ginger*
3 *egg whites, stiffly beaten*
Pastry for 2-crust pie

Mash the bananas very smooth. Stir in the sugar, butter, almonds, raisins, cinnamon, nutmeg, and ginger. Fold in the egg whites. Line a 9-inch pie plate with the pastry; turn the banana mixture into it. Cover with the remaining pastry. Bake in a preheated 425° oven for 35 minutes, or until browned. Cool on a cake rack. Serves 6–8.

Torta de Chocolate

CHOCOLATE TORTE

15 *squares semisweet chocolate*
⅔ *cup butter*
4 *egg yolks*
1 *teaspoon cinnamon*
1 *tablespoon sugar*
1 *tablespoon sifted cornstarch*
4 *egg whites*

Preheat oven to 425°.

Combine the chocolate and butter in the top of a double boiler; place over hot water until melted. Stir until smooth; cool for 10 minutes.

Beat the egg yolks until thick, then mix in the melted chocolate, cinnamon, sugar, and cornstarch. Beat the egg whites until stiff but not dry; fold into the chocolate mixture. Turn into an ungreased, 8-inch spring-form pan. Bake for 20 minutes, or until firm. Cool on a cake rack and remove sides of pan.

FROST WITH THE FOLLOWING:

> *4 squares semisweet chocolate*
> *3 tablespoons light corn syrup*
> *1½ teaspoons cognac*
> *¼ cup sliced Brazil nuts or almonds*

Combine the chocolate, syrup, and cognac in the top of a double boiler; place over hot water and stir until melted. Cool for 10 minutes; then ice the torte. Sprinkle the nuts on top. Serves 10–12.

 *Pastel Venezolano*

ALMOND TART

PASTRY SHELLS:

> *2 cups sifted flour*
> *½ teaspoon salt*
> *¼ cup confectioners' sugar*
> *½ pound butter*
> *1 egg, beaten*
> *¼ cup ice water*

[*over*]

Sift the flour, salt, and sugar into a bowl. Work in the butter with the hand; then work in the egg. Add just enough of the water to make a dough. Chill 2 hours. Roll out ¼ inch thick on a lightly floured surface and fit into 12 tart or muffin tins. Reserve pieces of pastry for tops. Preheat the oven to 425°.

FILLING:

> ¼ *pound butter*
> ½ *cup sugar*
> 4 *eggs*
> 1 *cup ground almonds*
> 2 *tablespoons cognac*
> 1 *teaspoon almond extract*

Cream the butter and sugar until fluffy. Beat in the eggs; then stir in the almonds, cognac, and almond extract. Spoon into the pastry shells. Roll out the remaining pastry very thin and cut into narrow strips. Place over the filling in a crisscross fashion. Bake for 20 minutes, or until browned and set. Cool and remove from pan. Serves 12.

One of the world's most delicious nuts, the Brazil nut, grows through most of tropical Central and South America, but particularly along the lush green banks of the Amazon River in Brazil. The tree itself is enormous, often rising over 100 feet, with leaves more than a foot in diameter. The nuts are found in a seed pod about the size of a large coconut and are so firmly sealed within that only a strong man using a heavy hammer can break open the seed pod. Within the pod are about twenty tightly packed nuts arranged something like the segments in a tangerine, with each nut enclosed in its own firm shell. Even finer is the paradise nut, with a more delicate flavor than the Brazil nut, which it resembles closely. However, owing to transportation difficulties, paradise nuts are rarely exported.

Torta de Castanha do Pará

BRAZIL-NUT CAKE

10 egg yolks
1 teaspoon instant coffee
1¾ cups superfine sugar
3 cups ground Brazil nuts
⅛ teaspoon salt
2 tablespoons cognac
2 tablespoons bread crumbs
10 egg whites
1½ cups heavy cream
2 tablespoons coffee essence
3 tablespoons confectioners' sugar
¼ cup slivered Brazil nuts

Preheat oven to 350°. Butter a 10-inch spring form and dust lightly with bread crumbs.

Beat the egg yolks and instant coffee; gradually add the sugar, beating until thick and light. Mix in the ground nuts, salt, cognac, and the 2 tablespoons bread crumbs. Beat the egg whites until stiff but not dry; fold into the nut mixture. Turn into the prepared pan. Bake for 50 minutes, or until a cake tester comes out clean. Cool on a cake rack before removing the pan.

Whip the cream; fold in the coffee essence and confectioners' sugar (if you don't have bottled coffee essence, dissolve 1 tablespoon instant coffee in 2 tablespoons water). Split the cake and spread cream between the layers and over the top and sides. Decorate with the slivered nuts. Serves 8–12.

Did you know that orchids are sometimes edible? Well, not all of them, of course. But the Vanilla planifolia *orchid combines beauty and the edible vanilla bean so familiar to those who cook.*

Torta De Pasa

RAISIN-FILLED CAKE

½ cup water
1 tablespoon cornstarch
⅞ cup sugar
1¼ cups seedless raisins
¾ cup chopped nuts
¾ cup (1½ sticks) butter
¾ cup dark brown sugar
3 eggs, beaten
3 cups sifted flour
2 teaspoons cream of tartar
2 teaspoons baking soda
¾ cup milk
1½ teaspoons vanilla extract

In a saucepan, mix the water, cornstarch, and ½ cup sugar. Cook over low heat, stirring constantly until thickened. Mix in the raisins and nuts. Cool while preparing the batter. Preheat oven to 375°.

Cream the butter, gradually adding the brown sugar and the remaining white sugar. Beat in the eggs until light and fluffy. Sift together the flour, cream of tartar, and baking soda. Add to the butter mixture alternately with the milk. Stir in the vanilla. Pour half the batter into a buttered 8-inch-square pan. Spread the raisin mixture over it and cover with the remaining batter. Bake for 35 minutes, or until a cake tester comes out clean. Cool on a cake rack. Cut into 2-inch squares. Makes 16.

Quesadilla de Arroz

RICE-FLOUR CUPCAKES

½ *pound sweet butter*
1 cup sugar
7 egg yolks
2 cups sifted rice flour or cornstarch
⅛ *teaspoon salt*
½ *teaspoon baking powder*
7 egg whites, stiffly beaten

Preheat oven to 375°.
Cream the butter, then beat in the sugar until fluffy. Add 1 egg yolk at a time, beating after each addition. Sift together the flour, salt, and baking powder. Stir into the butter mixture gradually. Fold in the egg whites.
Lightly butter about 16 cupcake tins and three quarters fill them with the batter. Bake for 15 minutes, or until browned and a cake tester comes out clean. Makes about 16.

There are so many oranges in Paraguay that no matter how many the local folk eat (and they do manage to consume plenty), so many remain that oranges are fed to cattle. The choicer ones are used in the delicious Orange Puffs.

Hojuelas de Naranja

ORANGE PUFFS

2 cups sifted flour
½ *teaspoon salt*
2 tablespoons sugar
3 tablespoons salad oil
¾ *cup orange juice*
Fat for deep frying

[over]

Sift together the flour, salt, and sugar; mix in the oil and just enough of the orange juice to form a dough. Roll out as thin as possible on a lightly floured surface. Cut into narrow strips, circles, or any shape you like.

Heat the fat to 375° and fry a few pieces at a time until browned. Drain and sprinkle with sugar. Makes about 3 dozen.

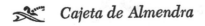 *Cajeta de Almendra*

ALMOND CUPS

2 *cups sugar*
1 *cup orange juice*
5 *egg whites*
¾ *cup ground almonds*

Cook the sugar and orange juice until a thread forms when a fork is lifted. Beat the egg whites until stiff but not dry. Gradually add the syrup, beating constantly until thick. Fold in the nuts thoroughly. Spoon into 2-inch paper cups.

Bake in a preheated 300° oven for 15 minutes. Cool. Makes about 15.

 *Roscas Almendra*

ALMOND DROPS

3 *egg whites*
4 *tablespoons sugar*
2 *tablespoons grated lemon rind*
2 *cups ground blanched almonds*

Preheat oven to 350°.

Beat the egg whites until stiff but not dry. Beat in the sugar, then fold in the rind and almonds. Put through a pastry bag in small twists or drop by the teaspoon onto a greased baking sheet. Bake for 10 minutes, or until delicately browned. Makes about 3 dozen.

❧ *Brazo Gitano*

CUSTARD-FILLED SPONGE ROLL

SPONGE ROLL:

> 5 *egg yolks*
> ⅓ *cup sugar*
> 5 *egg whites*
> ⅓ *cup sifted flour*
> ⅛ *teaspoon salt*
> ½ *teaspoon baking powder*

Preheat the oven to 425°. Grease a jelly-roll pan (11 x 18 inches), line with waxed paper, and grease the paper.

Beat the egg yolks, gradually adding the sugar; continue beating until light and fluffy. Beat the egg whites until stiff but not dry; heap on the egg yolks, but don't mix. Sift the flour, salt, and baking powder over the whites; fold in carefully but thoroughly. Turn into the prepared pan; spread evenly. Bake for 12 minutes. Carefully turn out onto a towel; peel the paper from the cake. Roll up the cake in the towel until cool.

CUSTARD FILLING:

> 6 *egg yolks*
> ¾ *cup sugar*
> ½ *cup sifted flour*
> 2 *teaspoons cornstarch*
> 3 *cups scalded milk*
> 2 *teaspoons vanilla extract*
> *Powdered sugar*

In a saucepan, beat together the egg yolks, sugar, flour, and cornstarch. Gradually add the hot milk, mixing steadily. Cook over low heat, mixing constantly, until thickened. Do not let boil. Remove from the heat and stir in the vanilla. Cool. Unroll the cake, spread filling on it, and roll up again. Cut into 1-inch slices. Sprinkle with powdered sugar. Makes 16.

   *Hinchares*

CREAM PUFFS

1 cup water
4 tablespoons butter
4 tablespoons sugar
1¼ cups flour
3 eggs
Fat for deep frying

Bring to a boil the water, butter, and sugar. Add the flour all at once, stirring steadily until mixture leaves the sides of the pan. Cool for 5 minutes; then beat in 1 egg at a time until smooth and glossy. Heat the fat to 375° and drop the mixture into it by the teaspoon (don't crowd the pan). Fry until browned and puffed. Drain well. Slit sides and fill with sweetened whipped cream. Makes about 2 dozen.

Pastelitos de Coco

COCONUT PASTRIES

2 cups sifted flour
½ teaspoon salt
½ teaspoon baking powder
¼ pound butter
4 tablespoons orange juice
1½ cups flaked coconut
1 tablespoon cornstarch
½ cup sugar
¾ cup light cream
2 egg yolks
3 tablespoons melted butter
1 egg white

Sift the flour, salt, and baking powder into a bowl; cut in the butter with a pastry blender or 2 knives. Mix in the orange juice until a ball of dough is formed. Chill for 1 hour.

Mix together the coconut, cornstarch, sugar, and cream. Cook over low heat, stirring constantly for 5 minutes. Add the egg yolks and melted butter gradually, stirring constantly. Stir over low heat for 2 minutes. Cool.

Roll out the dough on a lightly floured surface as thin as possible. Cut with a 3-inch cooky cutter. Place a tablespoon of the coconut mixture on half the circle and cover with the remaining circles. Seal the edges with a little water. Arrange on a baking sheet and brush with the egg white. Bake in a preheated 425° oven for 10 minutes, or until delicately browned. Cool on a cake rack. Makes about 2 dozen.

 Torta de Paste de Almendras

ALMOND-PASTE TART

1¼ cups (2½ sticks) butter
1¼ cups sugar
1 egg
1¾ cups sifted flour
2¼ cups ground almonds
1 teaspoon almond extract
2 tablespoons heavy cream

Preheat oven to 325°.

Cream the butter and sugar together. Mix in the egg, then the flour, 2 cups almonds, and the almond extract until smooth. Turn into a buttered 9-inch spring form. Brush the top with the cream and sprinkle with the remaining almonds. Bake for 50 minutes, or until delicately browned and a cake tester comes out clean. Cool before removing from pan. Serves 8–10.

Empanaditas de Crema

FRIED CREAM PASTRIES

FILLING:

> 5 *egg yolks*
> 1 *cup sifted flour*
> ⅞ *cup sugar*
> 2 *cups scalded milk*
> ¼ *pound butter*
> 1 *teaspoon vanilla extract*

Beat the egg yolks in a saucepan; stir in the flour and sugar until smooth. Gradually add the scalded milk, stirring constantly. Cook over low heat, mixing steadily, until thick and smooth. Mix in the butter and vanilla until melted. Cool while preparing the pastry dough.

PASTRY:

> 2 *cups sifted flour*
> ⅛ *teaspoon salt*
> 2 *tablespoons sugar*
> 2 *egg yolks, beaten*
> ¾ *cup milk*
> *Fat for deep frying*
> ½ *cup confectioners' sugar*

Sift the flour, salt, and sugar into a bowl. Mix in the egg yolks and milk until a soft dough is formed. Roll out ⅛ inch thick on a lightly floured surface. Cut into 4-inch circles or squares. Place a tablespoon of the cream mixture on each, fold over the dough, and press edges together with a little water, then with the tines of a fork.

Heat the fat to 360° and fry a few pastries at a time for 5 minutes, or until browned. Drain, sprinkle with confectioners' sugar, and serve hot or cold. Makes about 30.

☒ *Dulce de Almendras*

ALMOND CRISPS

CAKE:

>   *4 egg yolks*
>   *1 egg white*
>   *1 cup sugar*
>   *1 cup ground toasted almonds*
>   *2 teaspoons grated lemon rind*

Preheat oven to 275°. Butter an 8-x-8-inch baking pan and dust with flour.

Beat the egg yolks until thick. Beat the egg whites until peaks form; then beat in the sugar until stiff. Fold into the yolks with the almonds and lemon rind. Turn into the pan. Bake for 25 minutes, or until firm when pressed with the fingers. Cool, then turn out onto a baking sheet. Cover with the following meringue:

MERINGUE:

>   *¼ cup water*
>   *¾ cup sugar*
>   *3 egg whites*

Boil the water and sugar until a thread forms when a fork is lifted from the syrup. Beat the egg whites until stiff, then gradually beat in the syrup. Cover the top and sides of the cake and place in a 275° oven for 10 minutes, or until delicately browned. Cool and cut in strips. Serves 8–10.

Searchers for the world's most ideal climate would scarcely need to go farther than Quito, in Ecuador, a city of almost perpetual spring. Days are sunny and mild as a rule, and nights are cool and ideal for sleeping. The average temperature is 55 degrees every month of the year except August and September, when Quito gets very, very hot and the temperature jumps up to 56 degrees! *Buñuelos* and coffee provide a little much-needed warmth.

 Buñuelos

SWEET FRITTERS, ECUADORIAN MANNER

SYRUP:

> ·1 *cup dark brown sugar*
> 2 *tablespoons cornstarch*
> 1 *cup water*
> 2 *tablespoons butter*
> 2 *tablespoons heavy cream*
> 1 *teaspoon vanilla extract*

Mix the brown sugar and cornstarch in a saucepan; stir in the water. Cook over low heat, stirring constantly to the boiling point. Cook until thick, about 10 minutes, stirring occasionally. Mix in the butter, cream and, vanilla. Keep warm while preparing the fritters.

FRITTERS:

> 1 *cup water*
> ½ *cup sugar*
> 3 *tablespoons butter*
> 2 *tablespoons grated lemon rind*
> 1 *cup sifted cake flour*
> 3 *eggs*
> *Fat for deep frying*

Bring to a boil the water, sugar, butter, and lemon rind. Add the flour all at once, mixing until the dough leaves the sides of the pan. Cool for 5 minutes. Beat in 1 egg at a time, until the dough is shiny and smooth.

Heat the fat to 375°. Drop in the dough by the teaspoon. Fry until browned. Drain. Heap fritters in a bowl and pour the hot syrup over them. Serves 6–8.

Buñuelos de Banana

BANANA FRITTERS

4 bananas
4 egg yolks
3 egg whites
1½ teaspoons baking powder
3 tablespoons salad oil
½ cup powdered sugar

Buy very ripe bananas; mash smooth. Mix in the egg yolks, whites, and baking powder. Form tablespoons of the mixture into patties. Heat the oil in a skillet until it bubbles. Brown the patties on both sides. Drain, dip in the sugar, and serve hot. Serves 4.

Buñuelos de Almendras

FRIED ALMOND CRISPS

4 egg yolks
4 egg whites
2 cups sifted flour
½ teaspoon salt
3 tablespoons sugar
3 tablespoons ground almonds
Fat for deep frying   [over]

Beat the egg yolks until thick and light. Beat the egg whites until stiff but not dry, then mix with the yolks. Sift together the flour, salt, and sugar; mix in the nuts and add to the eggs. Mix until well blended. Break off small pieces and roll between the hands into finger lengths.

Heat the fat to 375° and fry a few at a time until browned. Drain well. Sprinkle with confectioners' sugar if desired. Makes about 3 dozen.

   *Tortilla de Banana*

BAKED BANANA DESSERT OMELET

5 tablespoons butter
4 bananas, sliced
6 egg yolks
1 teaspoon salt
¼ cup light cream
6 egg whites
½ cup sugar

Preheat the oven to 350°.

Melt 4 tablespoons butter in a skillet; sauté the bananas for 5 minutes, shaking the pan frequently. Beat the egg yolks, salt, and cream until light. Beat the egg whites until stiff but not dry; fold into the yolk mixture.

Butter a 1½-quart baking dish with the remaining butter; turn the mixture into it. Arrange the sautéed bananas on top. Bake for 15 minutes. Quickly sprinkle the sugar on top and bake 5 minutes longer, or until set. Serve at once. Serves 4–6.

In the Guianas, they distill a type of rum from sugar cane called Demerara, which is a mere 151 proof—that is 75½ per cent alcohol! It is believed to be the strongest liquor in the world.

Dulce de Guindas

CHERRIES IN SYRUP

2 cups water
4 cups sugar
3 tablespoons rum
2 pounds sour red cherries

Boil together the water and sugar for 10 minutes. Add the rum and cherries; cook over low heat until cherries look transparent. Chill. Use as a dessert or serve over ice cream. Makes about 1 quart.

Helado de Coco

COCONUT ICE CREAM

2 cups flaked coconut
2 cups milk
3 egg yolks
¾ cup sugar
2 cups heavy cream
½ cup fine grated coconut

Combine the flaked coconut and milk in a saucepan. Bring to a boil and let soak for 30 minutes. Press all the milk from the coconut and discard coconut. Beat the egg yolks and sugar in the saucepan; gradually add the coconut milk, stirring steadily to prevent curdling. Cook over low heat, stirring steadily until thickened. Do not let boil. Cool for 15 minutes.

Whip the cream and fold into the yolk mixture with the grated coconut. Turn into ice cube trays and freeze until sides become mushy. Beat until frothy and return to trays. Freeze until firm. Serves 6–8.

༄ Mousse de Chocolate

CHOCOLATE MOUSSE

3 squares unsweetened chocolate
1 tablespoon brewed coffee
4 egg yolks
½ cup sugar
½ teaspoon vanilla extract
4 egg whites
Whipped cream

Melt the chocolate in the coffee over hot water. Cool. Beat the
egg yolks and sugar until light and fluffy; mix in the melted
chocolate and vanilla. Beat the egg whites until stiff but not dry;
fold into the chocolate mixture. Turn into a 1½-quart mold or 6
individual serving dishes. Chill and serve with whipped cream.
Serves 6.

༄ Pudín de Almendras

ALMOND-RAISIN PUDDING

½ cup seedless raisins
½ cup dry sherry
3 eggs
1 cup sugar
2 cups light cream
2 cups blanched finely ground almonds
1 teaspoon cinnamon
¼ teaspoon nutmeg

Preheat oven to 350°.
Soak the raisins in the sherry for 20 minutes; drain. Beat the
eggs in a bowl; gradually beat in the sugar until light and fluffy.
Mix in cream, then almonds, cinnamon, nutmeg, raisins.
Spoon into 6 buttered custard cups. Set in a pan of warm water;
bake for 25 minutes, or until set and lightly browned on top.
Serve warm or ice cold, with whipped cream, if desired. Serves 6.

Dulce de Arroz

RICE-NUT DESSERT

1½ cups rice
4½ cups milk
1 teaspoon salt
¾ cup sugar
¾ cup ground almonds
3 egg yolks, beaten
Cinnamon

Wash the rice under running water. Combine with the milk and salt; let stand for 1 hour. Cook over low heat for 15 minutes. Cool for 10 minutes, then mix in the sugar, almonds, and egg yolks. Turn into a buttered baking dish. Bake in a preheated 350° oven for 20 minutes. Chill and sprinkle with cinnamon. Serves 4–6.

Arroz con Coco

COCONUT-RICE PUDDING

1 cup flaked coconut
1½ cups milk
1 cup rice
2 cups boiling water
½ teaspoon salt
½ cup brown sugar
1 teaspoon grated lime or lemon rind
Cinnamon

Bring the coconut and milk to a boil; let stand for 30 minutes. Press all the milk from the coconut and discard coconut.

Cook the rice in the boiling salted water for 15 minutes. Drain well. Combine with the coconut milk, brown sugar, and rind. Cook over low heat for 10 minutes, or until creamy. Pour into a mold or 6 individual dishes and chill. Sprinkle with a little cinnamon. Serves 6.

Arroz Zambito

FRUIT-AND-COCONUT DESSERT

2 cups raw rice
4½ cups water
⅛ teaspoon anise
1 teaspoon cinnamon
1 teaspoon salt
1½ cups dark brown sugar
¼ cup flaked coconut
¼ cup chopped walnuts
2 tablespoons seedless raisins
3 tablespoons butter

Wash the rice under running water. Bring 3½ cups water, the anise, cinnamon, and salt to a boil. Add the rice, cover, and cook over low heat for 15 minutes. Drain, if any water remains.

Combine the brown sugar with the remaining water; bring to a boil. Add the rice; cook over low heat for 10 minutes, stirring frequently. Mix in the coconut, walnuts, raisins, and butter. Cook 5 minutes longer. Serve very cold. Serves 6–8.

Bien-me-sabe: in Spanish, this means "I know it well," and is a familiar term referring to any family-style, simple dessert. It varies from cook to cook, and almost never means the same thing twice. Naturally a first-class hotel or restaurant would rarely condescend to put *bien-me-sabe* upon its menu, but it may be frequently encountered in small, provincial restaurants. *Bien-me-sabe* might then refer to a gelatin dessert, a cornstarch pudding, or possibly a custard.

 *Caramelo*

CARAMEL CUSTARD

½ *cup sugar*
6 *egg yolks*
¼ *teaspoon salt*
2 *cups milk*
1 *cup light cream*

Preheat oven to 375°.
Melt half the sugar and cook over low heat until light brown.
Divide among 8 custard cups.
Beat the egg yolks, salt, and remaining sugar; stir in the milk
and cream. Strain into the custard cups; set in a pan containing
2 inches of hot water. Bake for 30 minutes, or until a knife inserted in the center comes out clean. Cool and turn out, syrup
and all. Serves 8.

 *Quesilla de Piña*

PINEAPPLE CHEESE (CUSTARD)

1 *cup unsweetened pineapple juice*
¾ *cup granulated sugar*
6 *eggs*

Cook the juice and sugar over low heat for 15 minutes. Cool.
Pour 2 tablespoons of the syrup into a 1-quart baking dish and
turn to coat the sides.
Beat the eggs until light, then add the remaining syrup. Pour
into the prepared dish. Place in a shallow pan of hot water.
Bake in a 350° oven for 45 minutes, or until a knife inserted in
the center comes out clean. Cool, cover, and chill overnight. Carefully turn out and decorate with canned pineapple and whipped
cream. Serves 4–6.

✑ Crema Española

SPANISH CREAM

2 envelopes gelatin
4 cups milk
3 egg yolks
6 tablespoons sugar
3 egg whites
2 teaspoons vanilla extract

Soften the gelatin in ½ cup milk. Beat the egg yolks and half the sugar in a saucepan; mix in the gelatin mixture and the remaining milk. Cook over low heat, stirring steadily to the boiling point, but do not let it boil or the eggs will curdle.

Beat the egg whites and remaining sugar until stiff but not dry. Add the hot mixture and vanilla; beat until thoroughly mixed. Divide among 8–10 custard cups or pour into a 2-quart mold. Chill. Serves 8–10.

✑ Pan Dulce

SWEET BREAD

2 packages yeast
¼ cup lukewarm water
¼ cup milk, scalded and cooled
4½ cups sifted flour
¾ cup (1½ sticks) butter
½ cup sugar
3 eggs
2 egg yolks
2 tablespoons grated lemon rind
½ teaspoon salt
1 cup seedless raisins
½ cup chopped candied lemon peel
1 cup chopped nuts

Soften the yeast in the water for 5 minutes; mix in the milk and ½ cup flour. Cover and set aside in a warm place until risen and bubbly.

Cream the butter and sugar until fluffy. Beat in the eggs and yolks, then the lemon rind, salt, and enough of the remaining flour to make a soft dough. Knead until smooth and elastic, adding the raisins, candied lemon peel, and nuts at the same time. Cover and let rise in a warm place until double in bulk. Punch down and knead again. Place in an 8-x-12-inch loaf pan or divide between 2 4-x-10-inch loaf pans. Cover and let rise again until double in bulk. Bake in a preheated 375° oven—50 minutes for a large one, 35 minutes for small ones—or until browned and shrunk away from the sides of the pan. For a glossy top, brush with heavy cream before baking.

 Galletas de Nuences

NUT COOKIES

½ pound butter
2 cups dark brown sugar
2 eggs
1 teaspoon vanilla extract
3½ cups sifted flour
¼ teaspoon salt
1 teaspoon baking soda
1 cup chopped walnuts

Cream the butter, then beat in the brown sugar. Mix in the eggs and vanilla until smooth and fluffy. Sift together the flour, salt, and baking soda; add to the butter mixture. Work in the nuts. The dough should be very stiff. Form into 2 rolls, 1 inch in diameter. Wrap in foil or waxed paper and chill for 2 hours.

Preheat the oven to 375°. Slice the rolls very thin and place on a cooky sheet. Bake for 10 minutes. Makes about 6 dozen.

Note: Bake only the amount you require, and keep remaining dough in the refrigerator.

Brazilians are fond of slang, and have many short-cut expressions which everyone understands. Incidentally, not all of these are suitable in polite conversation. This love of short cuts and slang names has progressed to the kitchen, where classic Brazilian dishes have favorite names. For example, there's Baba de Moça, the Maiden's Kiss, a coconut dessert. How about Love in Pieces (Amor en Pedaços), an almond confection? Beijinhos de Ya-Ya means Mother-in-Law's Kisses, and is a lemon-coconut cooky which implies that mothers-in-law are highly regarded; but on the other hand there's Olho de Sogra, made with prunes, which translates into Mother-in-Law's Eye, which is none too flattering. Incidentally, ya-ya is the affectionate Brazilian word for mother-in-law, which often replaces the more formal sogra. But we think the prize name is Beijos de Cabocla, or Kisses of the Farmer's Daughter!

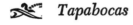 *Tapabocas*

SHERRY COOKIES

2 cups sifted flour
4 tablespoons sugar
¼ teaspoon salt
¼ pound butter
2 tablespoons cream cheese
1 egg, beaten
¼ cup sweet sherry

Preheat oven to 375°.
Sift together the flour, sugar, and salt. Work in the butter and cream cheese with the hand. Mix in the egg and sherry until a ball of dough is formed. Force through a cooky press in small spirals or shape by the teaspoon onto a baking sheet. Bake for 10 minutes, or until browned. Makes about 5 dozen.

Pastitas de Maíz

CORN-MEAL COOKIES

½ *pound butter*
1 cup sugar
1 cup corn meal

Preheat oven to 300°.
Cream the butter and sugar together; mix in the corn meal.
Shape into walnut-sized balls and arrange on a cooky sheet,
leaving 1 inch between each. Bake for 20 minutes, or until delicately browned. Makes about 3 dozen.

*During the sixteenth and seventeenth centuries, Buenos
Aires, the capital of Argentina, could hardly be recommended as a tourist spot. The city suffered from recurring
plagues, the water supply was foul, and there was danger
at every corner. Walking about after dark was extremely
hazardous, for robbers lurked at many crossroads. The
streets, if they could so be classified, consisted of muddy
roadways, with holes deep enough to swallow a horse and
carriage. No one moved at night without the assistance of
an armed guard, to ward off the anticipated forays of robbers and hoodlums. Today, tourists find an immaculate,
extremely modern city, filled with lovely parks, broad
boulevards, boasting a cosmopolitan, sophisticated population dedicated to the art of good living. More than any
other city in the Western Hemisphere, Buenos Aires has
been compared to Paris.*

One of the favorite jokes in Chile is that a local fruit, the poemo, *cannot be eaten by women. The* poemo *has a hard pulp which gradually dissolves in the mouth, and since women traditionally cannot keep their mouths closed long enough, it is said to be impossible for them to eat the* poemo.

 Alfajores de Almendras

ALMOND COOKIES, ARGENTINA

½ *pound butter*
1 cup sugar
3 eggs
2 tablespoons grated lemon rind
2 tablespoons cognac
¼ *teaspoon almond extract*
1 cup sifted flour
2 cups ground blanched almonds
4 tablespoons heavy cream
¾ *cup slivered almonds*

Cream the butter, gradually adding the sugar. Beat until fluffy. Add 1 egg at a time, beating well after each addition. Mix in the lemon rind, cognac, almond extract, flour, and ground almonds. Form into a ball and wrap in waxed paper or foil and chill 3–4 hours.

Roll out the dough on a lightly floured surface as thin as possible. Cut with a cooky cutter into any shapes. Transfer to a buttered baking sheet with a spatula. Brush with the cream and sprinkle with the slivered almonds. Bake in a preheated 375° oven for 12 minutes, or until delicately browned. Makes about 4 dozen 3-inch cookies.

⤞ *Dulce de Camote*

SWEET-POTATO CANDY

1 cup canned undrained, grated pineapple
2 cups mashed sweet potatoes
½ teaspoon salt
¼ teaspoon cream of tartar
2 cups brown sugar
⅔ cup boiling water
1 cup shelled almonds

Combine the pineapple, potatoes, and salt; cook over low heat, stirring steadily, for 5 minutes. Dissolve the cream of tartar and brown sugar in the boiling water; add to the potato mixture. Cook over low heat until a soft ball is formed when a drop is placed in cold water. Remove from the heat and beat until smooth and shiny. Mix in the almonds. Drop by the teaspoon onto a buttered surface. Chill. Makes about 6 dozen.

Do the Brazilians drink coffee? You bet they do, from morning until night! Upon arising, the breakfast cup is prepared with half coffee and half hot milk, called *café com leite*. But that's the end of milk in coffee, and for the rest of the day, Brazilians drink it black and very sweet (to American taste); this is *café preto*. If a Brazilian is waiting for a streetcar he walks to an outdoor café (and there is one on just about every street corner) and has a *café preto*. If he's waiting for his girl friend, and especially if he's waiting for his wife (who will probably be late), he drinks a *café preto*. If you meet a Brazilian friend on the street, you'll head directly for—yes, you guessed it—the twenty-third cup of coffee. Of course, *café preto* is served in an infinitesimally small cup, even smaller than our demitasse cup.

🐟 *Café com Leite*

COFFEE WITH HOT MILK

1½ cups boiling milk
1 tablespoon regular grind coffee
1 teaspoon sugar

Bring the milk and coffee to a boil in an enamel saucepan. Let stand in a warm place for 5 minutes. Strain and stir in the sugar; add a little more sugar if you wish.

The favorite drink of some 35 million South Americans is neither coffee nor tea—it's a locally produced beverage called *maté*. This holds true particularly for people in Brazil, Uruguay, Paraguay, Argentina, and Chile, where the average person drinks it from morning till night.

Maté, also called Paraguayan tea, grows on a bush which roughly resembles holly, the familiar Christmas plant. The leaves are picked, dried and later ground small, although there are many who prefer their *maté* in leaf form. The drink is prepared much like tea, but it is customary to brew it in a small gourd-shaped container and drink it through a straw called a *bombilla*. The color and flavor are strongly reminiscent of tea, but the taste is somewhat more astringent, or, some people think, more acidic. *Maté* may be drunk without sugar (*maté amargo*), or sweetened (*maté dulce*); many people add orange peel for additional flavor. *Maté* is obtainable at many American food-specialty shops and is interesting to try.

Maté Cocida

HOT MATÉ

In South America, *maté* is made in a gourd. It may also be made in a small teapot.

Place 2 tablespoons *maté* and 2 teaspoons sugar in the container. Add 1 cup hot, but not boiling, water. Let steep 5 minutes.

Maté Tetre

ICED MATÉ

3 *tablespoons* maté
3 *tablespoons sugar*
4¼ *cups boiling water*
1 *tablespoon lemon juice*

Mix the *maté* and sugar; add the boiling water. Cover and let stand for 20 minutes. Strain and add the lemon juice. Chill; then serve with ice cubes in tall glasses. Serves 4–6.

English Index

Almond cookies, Argentina, 252
  crisps, 239
  crisps, fried, 241–42
  cups, 234
  drops, 234
  -paste tart, 237
  -raisin pudding, 244
  tart, 229–30
Appetizers:
  avocado, 17
  avocado cocktail, 20
  avocado dip I, II, III, 18–19
  avocado-salad, 19
  crab-meat ramekins, 21
  fried pork bits, 20
  sardine stuffed eggs, 17
  seafood-cocktail sandwiches, 15
  shrimp in almond sauce, 16
  shrimp croquettes, 14
Argentina, 13, 25, 30, 81, 83–84, 94,
    116, 251, 254
Argentine thick chicken-and-vege-
    table soup, 27,
Avocado:
  appetizer, 17
  cocktail, 20
  dip I, II, III, 18–19
  -potato salad, 213–14
  -salad appetizer, 19
  salad, 12
    molded, 214
    Vera Cruz, 212–13
  sauce for fish, 221
  soup, cream of, 37
  stuffed, 215

Baked eggs, 48–49
Baked-potato-and-corn casserole, 170
Banana dessert omelet, baked, 242
  fritters, 241
  pie, 228
  tart, 227
Bananas, 227
Beans, 155
  black, 179
    and assorted meats, Brazilian,
      172–73
    and white, 175–76
  fried, with cheese, 177
  green:
    and potatoes, 201–2

in tomato sauce, 203–4
lentils:
  and bananas, 179–80
  with sausages, 177–78
  in tomato sauce, 176
and pork, Yucatán style, 173–74
red-bean soup, 41
re-fried, 175
See also Chick-peas
Bean salad, 216
Beef:
  batter-fried fillet of, Buenos Aires,
    86
  chipped, and vegetables, 99
  creole, 86–87
  meat-and-rice croquettes, 103
  meat-ball soup, 26
  meat balls with rice, 100
  meat loaf:
    spicy, 98
    Venezuelan, 96
  meat pie with potato crust, 102
  -and-rice hash, Paraguayan, 103
  steak. See Steak
  stuffed peppers, 95
  -and-vegetable stew, 91
  -vegetable stew, 97
  Venezuelan meat loaf, 96
  See also Steak
Beer, 87
Beverages. See under name of bev-
    erage
Black and white beans, 175–76
Black beans, 179
  and assorted meats, Brazilian, 172–
    73
Bolivia, 57, 108, 134–35, 170, 196
Bolivian fried chicken in corn-meal
    batter, 135
  pork casserole, 109
Brazil, 37–38, 57, 68, 72–73, 87–88,
    89, 98, 138, 161, 171–72, 211,
    230, 251, 253, 254
Brazilian black beans and assorted
    meats, 172–73
  shrimp-coconut stew, 67–68
Brazil-nut cake, 231
Broth:
  fish-and-tomato, 31–32
  Mexican meat balls in, 32

257

Foreign Index

SPANISH INTEREST TITLES
FROM HIPPOCRENE

SPANISH-ENGLISH/ENGLISH-SPANISH
Concise Dictionary (Latin American)
by Ila Warner

The vast majority of Spanish-speaking people in America come from Latin American countries. This dictionary meets the needs of these Hispanic Americans and anyone wishing to communicate in the same Spanish most Americans speak. Includes 8,000 entries with pronunciation.

500 pages, 4 x 6, 0-7818-0261-X
$11.95pb (258)

SPANISH-ENGLISH/ENGLISH-SPANISH
Dictionary of Computer Terms
by Alfredo U. Chiri

This dictionary features over 5700 English and Spanish computer terms. Common-sense pronunciation is included in both sections.

120 pages, 5 1/2 x 8 1/2, 0-7818-0148-6
$16.95 (036)

500 SPANISH WORDS AND PHRASES
Written and Edited by Carol Watson and Janet DeSaulles

This book uses colorful cartoons to teach children basic Spanish phrases and vocabulary.

32 pages, 8 x 10 1/4, color illustrations, 0-7818-0262-8
$8.95 (0017)

SPANISH VERBS: SER AND ESTAR
by Juan and Susan Serrano

Finally, a volume to eliminate the confusion concerning the two Spanish verbs for "to be."

220 pages, 5 1/2 x 8 1/2, 0-7818-0024-2
$8.95pb (292)

SPANISH-ENGLISH/ENGLISH-SPANISH
Practical Dictionary
by Arthur S. Butterfield

338 pages, 5 1/2 x 8 1/4, 0-7818-0179-6
$9.95pb (211)

MASTERING SPANISH

by Robert Clark

A useful tool for language learning, this method combines a full-size text with two audio cassettes allowing learners to hear proper pronunciation by native speakers, as they study the book.

Book
338 pages, 5 1/2 x 8 1/2, 0-7818-059-8
$11.95pb   (527)
2 Cassettes
0-87052-067-9, $12.95   (528)

MASTERING ADVANCED SPANISH

by Robert Clark

An advanced course of Spanish study utilizing the method of **Mastering Spanish**.

Book
326 pages, 5 1/2 x 8 1/2, 0-7818-0081-1
$14.95pb   (413)
2 Cassettes
0-7818-0089-7, $12.95

(All prices subject to change.)

TO PURCHASE HIPPOCRENE BOOKS contact your local bookstore, or write to: HIPPOCRENE BOOKS, 171 Madison Avenue, New York, NY 10016. Please enclose check or money order, adding $5.00 shipping (UPS) for the first book and $.50 for each additional book.

SPANISH FAMILY COOKBOOK
Juan and Susan Serrano

Who better to write the book on Spanish cookery than two native Spaniards and avid gourmands? In this guide to authentic Spanish cookery, Susan and Juan Serrano have culled over 250 of their favorite recipes from family menus and regional cuisine. The book covers each course of the Spanish meal, from *tapas* (appetizers) through *postres y pasteles* (desserts, cakes and pastries). Garnished with a generous sprinkling of personal anecdotes and cultural insights, the book explores old family recipes handed down over the years, practical adaptations of traditional cooking methods as well as some of the authors' more recent creations, and their versions of favorite Spanish dishes.

The recipes are seasoned with commentaries on regional variations, piquant observations on traditions and local customs, and explanations of curious Spanish words and culinary proverbs. Includes an entertaining and informative introduction to Spanish cuisine and indices in both English and Spanish.

247 pages 6 x 9

ISBN 0-7818-0193-1 $ 9.95pb (245)
ISBN 0-7818-0129-X $19.95cloth (249)

HIPPOCRENE LANGUAGE AND TRAVEL GUIDES

These guides provide an excellent introduction to a foreign country for the traveler who wants to meet and communicate with people as well as sightsee. Each book is also an ideal refresher course for anyone wishing to brush up on their language skills.

LANGUAGE AND TRAVEL GUIDE TO AUSTRALIA, by Helen Jonsen
Travel with or without your family through the land of "OZ" on your own terms; this guide describes climates, seasons, different cities, coasts, countrysides, rainforests, and the Outback with a special consideration to culture and language.
250 pages • $14.95 • 0-7818-0166-4 (0086)

LANGUAGE AND TRAVEL GUIDE TO FRANCE, by Elaine Klein
Specifically tailored to the language and travel needs of Americans visiting France, this book also serves as an introduction to the culture. Learn the etiquette of ordering in a restaurant, going through customs, and asking for directions.
320 pages • $14.95 • 0-7818-0080-3 (0386)

LANGUAGE AND TRAVEL GUIDE TO INDONESIA
A unique travel guide that balances useful travel information with essential phrases for getting around this beautiful country.
350 pages • $18.95 • 0-7818-0328-4 (0111)

LANGUAGE AND TRAVEL GUIDE TO MEXICO, by Ila Warner
Explaining exactly what to expect of hotels, transportation, shopping, and food, this guide provides the essential Spanish phrases, as well as describing appropriate gestures, and offering cultural comments.
224 pages • $14.95 • 0-87052-622-7 (503)

LANGUAGE AND TRAVEL GUIDE TO RUSSIA, by Victorya Andreyeva and Margarita Zubkus
Allow Russian natives to introduce you to the system they know so well. You'll be properly advised on such topics as food, transportation, the infamous Russian bath house, socializing, and sightseeing. Then, use the guide's handy language sections to be both independent and knowledgeable.
293 pages • $14.95 • 0-7818-0047-1 (0321)

LANGUAGE AND TRAVEL GUIDE TO UKRAINE (Revised)
by Linda Hodges and George Chumak
Written jointly by a native Ukrainian and an American journalist, this guide details the culture, the people, and the highlights of the Ukrainian experience, with a convenient (romanized) guide to the essentials of Ukrainian
266 pages • $14.95 • 0-7818-0135-4 (0057)

HIPPOCRENE HANDY DICTIONARIES

For the traveler of independent spirit and curious mind, this practical series will help you to communicate, not just to get by. Common phrases are conveniently listed through key words. Pronunciation follows each entry and a reference section reviews all major grammar points. *Handy Extras* are extra helpful—offering even more words and phrases for students and travelers.

ARABIC
$8.95•0-87052-960-9 (463)

CHINESE
$8.95•0-87052-050-4 (347)

CZECH EXTRA
$8.95•0-7818-0138-9 (063)

DUTCH
$8.95•0-87052-049-0 (323)

FRENCH
$8.95•0-7818-0010-2 (155)

GERMAN
$8.95•0-7818-0014-5 (378)

GREEK
8.95•0-87052-961-7 (464)

HUNGARIAN EXTRA
$8.95•0-7818-0164-8 (002)

ITALIAN
$8.95•0-7818-0011-0 (196)

JAPANESE
$8.95•0-87052-962-5 (466)

KOREAN
$8.95 • 0-7818-0082-X (438)

PORTUGUESE
$8.95 • 0-87052-053-9 (324)

RUSSIAN
$8.95 • 0-7818-0013-7 (371)

SERBO-CROATIAN
$8.95 • 0-87052-051-2 (328)

SLOVAK EXTRA
$8.95 • 0-7818-0101-X (359)

SPANISH
$8.95 • 0-7818-0012-9 (189)

SWEDISH
$8.95 • 0-87052-054-7 (345)

THAI
$8.95 • 0-87052-963-3 (468)

TURKISH
$8.95 • 0-87052-982-X (375)

Spanish Literature
from Hippocrene . . .

MISERICORDIA
Benito Perez Galdos
translated by Charles De Salis

Set among the poor of Madrid, this novel grapples with the
problem of goodness.
320 pages   1-873782-85-2
$16.95pb (0465)

TREASURY OF SPANISH LOVE POEMS, QUOTATIONS AND PROVERBS
in Spanish and English
edited and translated by Juan and Susan Serrano

A bilingual gift collection of popular Spanish love poems,
spanning eight centuries. Words from De La Vega, Garcia
Lorca and Calderon offer insight into the Spanish perspective
on romance.
128 pages   0-7818-0358-6
$11.95hc (0589)

Self-Taught Audio Language Courses

Hippocrene Books is pleased to recommend Audio-Forum self-taught language courses. They match up very closely with the languages offered in Hippocrene dictionaries and offer a flexible, economical and thorough program of language learning.

Audio-Forum audio-cassette/book courses, recorded by native speakers, offer the convenience of a private tutor, enabling the learner to progress at his or her own pace. They are also ideal for brushing up on language skills that may not have been used in years. In as little as 25 minutes a day — even while driving, exercising, or doing something else — it's possible to develop a spoken fluency.

Portuguese Self-Taught Language Courses

Continental Portuguese in Three Months 4 cassettes (4 hr.), 160-p. text, $69.95. Order #HPG10.

Brazilian Portuguese Vol. I 16 cassettes (19 hr.), 783-p. text, $215. Order #HP151.

Brazilian Portuguese Vol. II 18 cassettes (16 hr.), 618-p. text, $245. Order #HP180.

From Spanish to Brazilian Portuguese 2 cassettes (2 hr.), 91-p. text, $45. Order #HSP50.

All Audio-Forum courses are fully guaranteed and may be returned within 30 days for a full refund if you're not completely satisfied.

You may order directly from Audio-Forum by calling toll-free 1-800-243-1234.

For a complete course description and catalog of 264 courses in 91 languages, contact Audio-Forum, Dept. SE5, 96 Broad St., Guilford, CT 06437. Toll-free phone 1-800-243-1234. Fax 203-453-9774.

Self-Taught Audio Language Courses

Hippocrene Books is pleased to recommend Audio-Forum self-taught language courses. They match up very closely with the languages offered in Hippocrene dictionaries and offer a flexible, economical and thorough program of language learning.

Audio-Forum audio-cassette/book courses, recorded by native speakers, offer the convenience of a private tutor, enabling the learner to progress at his or her own pace. They are also ideal for brushing up on language skills that may not have been used in years. In as little as 25 minutes a day — even while driving, exercising, or doing something else — it's possible to develop a spoken fluency.

Spanish Self-Taught Language Courses

Programmatic Spanish, Vol. I 12 cassettes (17 hr.), 464-p. text, manual, $185. Order #HS101. *Workbook for Spanish, Vol. I,* 128-p., $7.95. Order #HS990.

Programmatic Spanish, Vol. II 8 cassettes (12 hr.), 614-p. text, manual, $155. Order #HS121. *Workbook for Spanish, Vol. II,* 201-p., $14.95. Order #HS995.

Basic Spanish Advanced Level Part A, Units 31-45 12 cassettes (13 hr.), 614-p. text, $185. Order #HS153.

Basic Spanish Advanced Level Part B, Units 46-55 12 cassettes (12½ hr.), 472-p. text, $185. Order #HS170.

Medical Spanish (Beginning Course) 12 cassettes (11½ hr.), 256-p. text, 29-p. Listener's Guide, $195. Order #HMS20.

Business Spanish (Intermediate Course) 6 cassettes (6 hr.), 162-p. text, $175. Order #HS24300.

All Audio-Forum courses are fully guaranteed and may be returned within 30 days for a full refund if you're not completely satisfied.

You may order directly from Audio-Forum by calling toll-free 1-800-243-1234.

For a complete course description and catalog of 264 courses in 91 languages, contact Audio-Forum, Dept. SE5, 96 Broad St., Guilford, CT 06437. Toll-free phone 1-800-243-1234. Fax 203-453-9774.